The 20 British Prime Ministers
of the 20th century

Salisbury

ERIC MIDWINTER

HAUS PUBLISHING · LONDON

First published in Great Britain in 2006 by
Haus Publishing Limited
26 Cadogan Court
Draycott Avenue
London SW3 3BX

www.hauspublishing.co.uk

A CIP catalogue record for this book is available from the British Library

ISBN 1-904950-54-X

Designed by BrillDesign
Typeset in Garamond 3 by MacGuru Ltd
info@macguru.org.uk

Printed and bound by Graphicom, Vicenza

Front cover: John Holder

Contents

Introduction: The Disregarded Premier

The General Holidays Bill of 1871 was a measure introduced by the Liberal politician, Sir John Lubbock, and it was passed with surprising ease, given that a more modest proposal had failed only three years previously. It provided for three extra annual holidays on Easter Monday, Whit Monday and the first Monday in August. 'Saint Monday' was the day when workers took what, in modern parlance, would be termed 'sickies', so Monday was the pragmatic choice, and the first-ever such holiday was celebrated on Whit Monday 1871. Hitherto only Good Friday and Christmas Day had been public holidays for everyone. In the less stringent decades of pre-Victorian economic laxity, the staff of the Bank of England had had 42 separate days but these had been reduced to 18 days by 1830 and then to four in 1834.

When the General Holidays Bill was at its committee stage in the House of Lords it received the crucial support of Lord Salisbury, in part because he did have some little conscience about easing the lot of the working man, in part because it was a scheme about which the sitting Liberal government, to which the Conservative peer was in opposition, remained unenthusiastic. The legal thrust of the bill was to ensure that all banks would close on these days, with the anticipated consequence of all businesses following suit. Thus Lord Salisbury suggested they be called 'Bank Holidays' – and so they were and they have brought some refreshment to the busy lives of millions.

This is probably Lord Salisbury's chief claim to a place in popular lore, but it is unlikely that many of those sunning themselves on the beaches or, a likelier fate, steaming in traffic jams on August Bank Holiday are aware of their benefactor. Nobody thought to call them 'Salisbury Days'; indeed, had they hinted at such a populist notion, the patrician Lord Salisbury would have been sorely offended. Other politicians have been thus eponymously adopted. Examples include the Gladstone bag; the Churchill tank or College; the Belisha beacon, after Leslie Hore-Belisha, Minister of Transport 1934–7, and the Anderson shelter, after Sir John Anderson, Home Secretary 1939–40. More recently there have been 'Baker Days', for in-service teacher training, after one of Margaret Thatcher's Education Secretaries, Kenneth Baker, and the proposal that extra-time schooling should be called 'Kelly Hours', after Tony Blair's Education Secretary, Ruth Kelly.

But there were to be no 'Salisbury Days'. In a nutshell that encapsulates much about the man, his public face and his historical account. Given that he was Prime Minister three times and for a joint period of over 13 years, he is the least well remembered of long-serving premiers. He is something of a forgotten man. Curiously, the rule-proving exception to the case occurred when, in 1890, the capital of Southern Rhodesia was founded and named Salisbury after the Prime Minister, who was closely associated with imperial policy and whose family had 80,000 acres of farmland in Rhodesia. First, within a generation, many people, had they bothered to think about it, would have assumed it was named after the cathedral city, as was Salisbury, North Carolina. Second, adding injury to insult, with the emergence of the independent republic of Zimbabwe in 1980, and a good riddance to imperialist vestiges, the city was renamed Harare.

For much of the 20th century, Lord Salisbury was, for those with but a general interest in political history, squeezed into anonymity between the competing giants, Gladstone and Disraeli, and the flamboyant David Lloyd George. Even as late as the 1950s, working men, in receipt of national insurance payments, would speak of collecting their 'Lloyd-George', acknowledging his ministerial hand in that Edwardian reform. Few memorials exist to applaud the work of the late Victorian Conservative leader and Lord Salisbury has long been a grey figure, chiefly remembered only by specialists in the field.

There can be little doubt that he would have preferred it that way. He shunned the limelight and did not play to the political gallery, not so much perhaps out of modesty but from hauteur. He scorned the trappings of rulership, possibly out of a decent sensibility of their emptiness, possibly because they had come so easily to him that he scarcely valued them. Lord Salisbury, born to the governmental purple, was, in regard of such baubles, akin to the plutocrat who was asked the cost of his yacht – if you have to ask, was his lofty reply, you can't afford it.

The mismatch between his length of service as Prime Minister and the slight mark he has left on the historical consciousness of the nation is the central key to an examination of his life and work. This book is basically an attempt to answer the question as to whether the public, taking Lord Salisbury at his own self-assessment, have been justified in consigning him to the dusty footnotes of the collective historical memory, or whether recent energetic endeavours to reconstruct him as a mighty and imposing personage, yet sadly misjudged and ignored, offer a more truthful interpretation.

Part One

THE LIFE

Chapter 1: From Noble Birth to Sitting Member

Among 20th century prime ministers, and even allowing for Winston Churchill's spirited ancestry, Lord Salisbury's antecedents were the most portentous in terms of likely political success. The Cecil family were originally of Welsh stock, hence, apparently, the rather twee pronunciation of 'Cecil' to rhyme with – to borrow from another kingdom's lore – 'thistle'. They provided the Tudors with faithful service. David Cecil fought with Henry VII at the decisive Battle of Bosworth Field in 1485 and was made a Yeoman of the Guard, his reward an estate in the Stamford area. His great grandson was the famed William Cecil, later Lord Burghley, the wise and perceptive advisor to Elizabeth I, while his son, Robert Cecil, replaced him and was instrumental in the safe transfer of monarchical power to James I on the death of the Queen in 1603. He was heavily involved in the 1605 Gunpowder Plot, some say as anxious guardian, others say as manipulative agent.

It was he who was created Earl of Salisbury and who exchanged his Lincolnshire estate for the crown land of Hatfield, in Hertfordshire, where, of course, the young Princess Elizabeth had awaited with some trepidation news of her accession to the throne. There he began the building of the Jacobean stately home that would one day be Lord Salisbury's opulent dwelling.

The fourth Earl found himself stranded on the wrong side when, at the time of the Glorious Revolution in 1689, he had backed the Roman Catholic James II against the Protestant contender, William of Orange. This Whig settlement introduced the real beginnings of a constitutional monarchy. The fourth Earl's preference for the *status quo* became the regular stance of the Cecils, as might be expected of such a longstanding landowning family. James Cecil, Lord Salisbury's grandfather, was an active Tory and Lord Chamberlain during the stirring times of the late 18th century; indeed, he was made a Marquess by George III in the climactic year of 1789. His son, also James, Lord Salisbury's father, was also a vigorous upholder of the landed interest. He was opposed to parliamentary reform and, unsurprisingly, Robert Peel's brave overthrow of the protectionist Corn Laws in 1846, whilst he served in a couple of Tory ministries in the 1850s.

It is worthwhile dwelling for a moment on this centuries-old lineage of traditional attachment to land and class with its concomitant obsessive wariness of change. Given the strength of that heritage, it would have been as remarkable if Lord Salisbury had become an adherent of Karl Marx (whose *Das Kapital* was published in 1867, the year Lord Salisbury spoke forcefully, as to the manner born, against Disraeli's parliamentary reform bill) as it would have been had one of Saddam Hussein's sons transpired to be a paid-up member of Amnesty International. Lord Salisbury was not to disappoint the watching shades of his aristocratic forebears.

Lord Salisbury was born at Hatfield House on 3 February 1830 and he was christened Robert Arthur Talbot Gascoyne-Cecil, the hyphen introducing the maiden name of his mother, Frances Gascoyne, whose rich family had brought increased wealth to the Cecil domain. The Duke of Wellington was his godfather. His birth and well being were important to the Cecil line, for the heir, his elder brother, James, Viscount Cranborne, was severely disabled and a second son had died in infancy. There were two much older sisters and one much younger brother, leaving 'Bobby' an isolated figure, never very strong physically and subject to mental depression. Nor was this condition helped by the death of his mother in 1839, when he was nine. Incidentally, and in the hope of avoiding undue confusion, the subject of this study will be referred to as 'Lord Salisbury' throughout, even in these opening pages before, of course, he had succeeded to the earldom.

Being born with a silver spoon in the mouth is no guarantee of a golden childhood idyll, however. Lord Salisbury's high-handed father, the second Marquess, subjected his son to a schooling of abject misery. After being whacked and starved from the age of six by the local vicar who took in tiny boarders, and following a rather more pleasant experience at a Devonshire school, he then went to Eton, aged ten, in 1840. Although Thomas Arnold had begun his celebrated headmastership of Rugby School in 1828, his governing text the primacy of 'Godliness and good learning', his reforming message was as yet unheeded by the public

Eton College in Windsor, Berkshire, was founded in 1440 by King Henry VI to provide free education for 70 poor scholars who would then go on to further their education at King's College, Cambridge. One of the country's most prestigious public schools, it has educated 18 prime ministers including Sir Robert Walpole, William Pitt the Elder and the Duke of Wellington. More recently Princes William and Harry attended the College.

schools that were 'essentially self-governing schoolboy republics, run by a prefectorial elite, in which the teachers rarely intervened'. In practice and habit, they were violent and debauched.

The new Etonian did not fit in well and refused to conform, especially to the code whereby clever pupils were coerced into doing the translations for older, lazier and less brainy boys. He was bullied hour after hour by a gang of ten or more; burnt with a candle; spat on and kicked; pelted and driven from meals; his possessions were damaged and destroyed, the constant beatings leaving him 'aching in every joint' and forced to hide in corners, without food, until the house had settled down for the night. He wrote to his father: *I know that you do not like complaints and I have tried to suppress them and conceal all this, but you are the only person to whom I can safely confide these things. Really now Eton has become insupportable. I am bullied from morning to night without ceasing.*[1] Young Robert was so terrorised that, eventually and after pitiful complaints, he was taken away in 1845 in a state of nervous and physical collapse. Thereafter he was tutored privately at Hatfield House, but the damage to heart and mind was done. He went up to Christ Church, Oxford, in 1847, and there, in a hot-bed of High Toryism and High Anglicanism, he felt more at home, although his repressed and lonesome childhood left him lacking in those cheery traits which enliven undergraduate existence. Studious in mode and active in the Oxford Union debates, life for him was much less of a trial, but, unluckily, ill-health, possibly the consequence of the horrors of Eton, felled him. He left after two years, with nothing more illustrious than an honorary fourth class degree in mathematics, little more than a glorified certificate of attendance.

Really now Eton has become insupportable. I am bullied from morning to night without ceasing.

SALISBURY TO HIS FATHER

It was a poor and inapt reward, for Lord Salisbury was, in fact, an extremely clever young man. Lonely hours in the Hatfield House library and even among the miseries of school, as well as during his six Oxford terms, had equipped him with a formidable knowledge. He had mastered modern languages, in addition to the classics and theology, while he developed a lifelong and practical interest in the sciences. One of the saddest aspects of the letter he wrote to his father describing his treatment at the hands of Etonian brutes was its elegance of phrasing, as if the milksop, George Arthur, in *Tom Brown's Schooldays*, published in 1857, had written home outlining the brutal antics of the bully Flashman. Indeed, in 1853, when his health had improved, he took the stiff examinations for and was elected to a Prize Fellowship of All Souls College, Oxford, something of a citadel of profound scholarship.

Lord Salisbury's was a redoubtable intellect, trained, indeed, self-trained to a nicety. Whatever abuse opponents might fling at him then or critics now, there should be no denial of his mental powers, even if one might question the purposes to which he addressed them. If Benjamin Disraeli or Winston Churchill might be judged as being the brightest intelligence to have led the Conservative Party, Lord Salisbury might be assessed as being the keenest intellect so to do. Left-wing detractors might submit the corollary that the competition in either of those categories is far from brisk, but, nonetheless, it is a salutary reminder to them that their antagonists are not invariably feeble-minded.

In the meanwhile, the doctors, as was often the response in Victorian times when the well-to-do were sick, prescribed a long overseas trip to allow him to recuperate. Thus in 1851 he embarked on a journey of almost two years, and for all the many discomforts naturally associated with such an undertaking, his physical health was largely repaired by this adventure. His choice of destinations – the British colonies in South Africa, Australia and New Zealand – is interesting, for he deliberately selected areas where his experiences would inform his later policies on imperial matters. It was as much a fact-finding mission as a health cruise, and much of what he found amid those rapacious and bustling young settlements sickened and appalled him. It used to be said of National Service in the 1940s and 1950s that one learned more in three days in a barrack room than one did in three years at college, and Lord Salisbury's equivalent of the modern 'gap year' certainly had something of this effect.

The vulgarities and depravities of colonial existence and the failures of religion in the imperial domains reinforced his view, formed through his boyhood traumas, that humankind was, with some few exceptions, decidedly unpleasant. The degradation of Melbourne, added to the barbarism of Eton, left him forever pessimistic about the happy progress of man, with only the otherworldly consolations of the Christian faith offering any faint hope. Like several of his ancestors, Lord Salisbury is said to have suffered from depression, but it is difficult to guess now how much of that was clinical and how much self-induced by gloomy forebodings. He took very literally the Prayer Book funeral service description of the human's 'vile body'. Rather as those with a persecution complex may sometimes be the victims of actual persecution, there may have been both cause and effect at work. Perhaps, with Lord Salisbury, the clinically morbid personality and the conscious belief in the ignobility of humanity locked together in a downward spiral of glumness.

He arrived home in 1853. Putting aside thoughts both of the Bar and the Church, those conventional career props for sons other than heirs of landed families, he opted for the political sphere. His initial reason, one that would endure throughout his long political life, was to join battle on behalf of the Anglican Church and its co-partner, the existing state, against the forces of secularism and subversion. Lord Salisbury was no superficial adherent of Anglicanism, going through the motions of its rituals for the sake of appearances. His daughter, Gwendolen, wondered aloud in her father's prolix biographical volumes, the first published in 1921, about his seeking for spiritual comfort amidst the morose days of his youth. It does seem that, starved of affection and alone, he turned and never strayed from an unquestioning acceptance of the impenetrability of the Godhead. Along with his academic prowess, this deeply-felt belief in the existence and yet the infinite mystery of a supernatural being was to be very much part of his political make-up.

True to his Oxford upbringing, he rejoiced in the sacramental dignities of High Church veneration and was wary of modernistic Anglican and out-and-out Nonconformist sects, as well as of the earthly ambitions of Rome. It is interesting that, like a good Victorian Tory, he objected to the Roman Catholic practice of the confessional as an invasion of family privacy, especially when this meant priests lasciviously sharing secrets with one's wife and daughters. His time at Oxford had coincided with the later days of Tractarianism, otherwise known as 'the Oxford Movement', the crusade led by the likes of Edward Pusey and John Keble. The campaign had been weakened by the conversion of J H Newman to Rome, but Lord Salisbury firmly adhered to the 'tracts' published in the hope of restoring the pre-Reformation traditions of the Church and reviving its spiritual potency in the face of scientific and secular advances.

Throughout his life he stuck firmly to an almost Erastian creed, believing that, if secular power could not be quite subordinate to ecclesiastical bidding, there should be a large measure of official alliance. Salisbury's principal biographer,

Andrew Roberts, asserts that the Victorian statesman was in main part responsible for the aphorism that the Church of England was 'the Tory party at prayer'.[2] Although there were other more generally determining factors at work, including the Liberal Party's own contrary identification with religious dissent, there is much truth in this opinion. Lord Salisbury came closer to probably any other premier, let alone those just of the 20th century, to being a theocrat. This much did he have in common with the ultra-conservative leaders of some modern Islamic states. At an individual level, it could, then, be confidently asserted that Lord Salisbury was, among the score of 20th-century premiers, the most sincerely and profoundly attached to a religious creed and doctrine. Probably only William Gladstone comes close to emulating his devout belief among the entire host of British prime ministers.

Here, then, was Lord Salisbury, still officially Lord Robert Gascoyne-Cecil, on the threshold of his doggedly influential career, having fully reached manhood – he was aged 23 – and, for the first time in his life, in something more like reasonable health. He did, however, continue to suffer what he called his 'nerve storms' and became and remained something of a hypochondriac. Among the catalogue of 'Victorian values' should always be listed valetudinarianism.

The advent of manhood had been betokened by a late upshooting in height. Lord Salisbury was 6ft 4in tall, already showing signs of his later stoop and incipient bulkiness. Short-sighted, melancholy eyes stared expressively from his rather sad, woebegone but by no means unattractive countenance. There were, too, already signs of baldness, but, as yet, his hair was dark and luxuriant, culminating in thick sideburns. As the baldness spread, the beard and moustache was allowed to sprout as if in hirsute compensation, so that, eventually, he would sport a beard that his near contemporary, the cricketer, W G Grace, might have envied.

Historians dabble at some hazard in the murky puddles of psychology. We have noted how some of his biographers have explained Lord Salisbury's unmitigated dogma of the imperfectability of man as being the consequence of the admittedly nasty experiences of his boyhood and teenage years. Certainly from that time he never deviated from a conviction that, unless redeemed by religion, humanity would, individually and collectively, choose evil over good. However, one might point to other cases where happier thoughts have prevailed in spite of corrosive formative conditions. It is difficult to determine where childhood influences and personality traits, such as a tendency towards depressiveness, are, if ever, overruled by genuinely objective and rational thinking.

Perhaps one should pay Lord Salisbury the compliment of accepting that his conjoined religio-political creed was the result of his own witting thought; it is undeniable that he studied and thought strenuously and deeply about these matters. That said, it is hard to ignore the confluence of determinants. He was the scion of one of the nation's great estates, his famous ancestors wedded to the preservation of the monarchy, of the peerage, of the landed interest and of the established church. Yet he had suffered what, had he endured it in the inner-city desolation of the late 20th century, might have been called a deprived childhood. The combination is fearsome. It is difficult to avoid the conclusion that, by nurture and by nature, he was inexorably and pessimistically committed to the cause of anti-progress and a resistance to change.

That this was self-serving is evident enough; it was manifestly improbable that the rich aristocratic landowner would be the first to call for equality and democracy. Their owners burnt few, if any, chateaux during the French Revolution. Nonetheless, unlike some defenders of ancient regimes, Lord Salisbury believed sincerely enough that it was in the general rather than just in the class interest that the old way should be preserved, and he was prepared to back his doctrine on the base of religious precepts. Even allowing for a natural tendency to rationalise his position as an obvious winner in the game of life, it was this element of objectivity in his thinking that helped make Lord Salisbury so impressive a political operator. Because he had a firm frame of theological reference, rather than just a batch of woolly slogans, he found himself able to manoeuvre with some facility. Being surefooted and certain in his creed enabled him thus to be dextrous in its everyday political application.

It was with this heritage and with this compound of talents that the young lordling turned his attentions to Parliament.

Chapter 2: From Stamford to Constantinople

About this time Lord Salisbury had two strokes of good fortune. One was in the public sphere. No sooner had he arrived home from his lengthy voyage, utterly decided upon a parliamentary career, than an unexpected vacancy occurred in the Stamford division. In spite of the inroads made by the seminal 1832 Reform Act into the practice of 'rotten' boroughs, the two members for Stamford remained in the 'pocket' of the local bigwig, the Marquess of Exeter, owner of the neighbouring Burghley estates and, through that Cecil connection, a kinsman of Lord Salisbury. The seat was made available to him in 1853. He represented the seat for 15 years, until his elevation to the House of Lords in 1868. At each election he was returned unopposed and is the last British prime minister never to have contested in a constituency battle. No one ever actually voted directly for Lord Salisbury for appointment to any political office he held.

Nor did he much seek the adulation, let alone the opinions, of those he represented, once privately confiding in a shuddering aside that he regarded importuning constituents as *vermin of that kind*, not a dissimilar comment to that made, rather more publicly, by Aneurin Bevan about Tories in the post-1945 years. Lord Salisbury made his maiden speech in the April of 1854, speaking caustically, as was his wont, against mild plans to update the funding of the University of Oxford. He took his duties seriously. The fact that he ventured into the Commons with but the mandate of the Marquess of Exeter to justify his entry did not deter him nor, at the other extreme, persuade him to live a dilettante political existence. He believed that a system that ensured those responsible for large-scale property became legislators was a righteous one and he worked hard enough, even at the risk of his health.

His father could not secure for him even a minor posting on the Privy Council and he turned down, on the grounds of its undue expense, the governorship of Moreton Bay, the later Queensland. But he soon established his credentials as an expert on foreign affairs, scornfully protesting in the House of Commons at the need for and conduct of the Crimean War (1854–6) and arguing that the opportunity to resolve the problem of the Ottoman Empire had been missed. He felt the pro-Turk, anti-Russian attitude of the then government was too unbalanced; as ever in his conduct of both foreign and imperial affairs, he thought that the steady pendulum was the mode most likely to secure British interests.

Such was his good luck in the public sphere. In the private sphere he was fortunate to marry with a great degree of contentment. The story of his nuptials is the stuff of a second-tier Victorian 'railway' novel of the kind made available by W H Smith, later to be a colleague of Lord Salisbury in Conservative Cabinets. The tale begins with his father's second marriage in 1847 to Lady Mary Sackville-West. They were to have five children, bringing the older Salisbury's score to ten, and, in consequence, he felt the need to milk his first wife's trust of money intended for her children. It was against this canvas of ill feeling and filial sniping that a friend of Lady Mary's visited Hatfield in 1856; she was Georgina Alderson, the daughter of a lawyer, Sir Edward Alderson, a distinctly middle-class figure of no pretentious wealth.

Lord Salisbury fell in love with her, having had, as far as any records indicate, no close contact beforehand with any other woman. There were even hints that she had deliberately set her cap at him. She was, at 29, three years older than her ardent suitor and, an obvious attraction for him, she shared his Tractarian leanings in religious belief, and was a woman of sprightly intelligence. Torn between the calls of chivalry and truth, the historian must concede that Georgina was no glamorous beauty, being somewhat dumpy of figure and doughy of feature. Like her husband-to-be, she had little or no interest in fashion or the high life. What she did have was the inestimable gift of lifting Lord Salisbury out of his interminable depressions, suggesting that, all along, his black moods were caused more by the lack of intimate companionship than deep-rooted clinical symptoms. Sometimes imprudent and tactless, she never spared herself in loyal support of her husband, both in private, by way of providing social comfort for one who found himself strangely ill at ease in any company, and in public, as the down-to-earth hostess of his necessary political gets-together.

That was the future. In the meanwhile, there was the family feud. Lord Salisbury's stepmother was cross with her erstwhile friend for abusing her hospitality by such carryings on, while her husband was aghast at the thought that his son was, unlike himself, not marrying for money. Given her Ritualistic creed, he also feared she might cross to Rome and that Hatfield, most definitively Protestant of large estates, might fall, in the next generation, into papist claws. On becoming an MP, Lord Salisbury had been given £100 a year by his father, plus £300 a year from the interest on his mother's estate of £10,000. The irate pater refused to consider any further financial settlement or any offer of accommodation at Hatfield. The family mainly sided with the father, as, in ironic Marxian fashion, economic dictates ruled over romantic notions.

In perhaps the one hazardous throw of a life largely confined to cautious decisions, Lord Salisbury defied the paternal wrath. In November 1856 he wrote to his father: *The persons who will cut me because I marry Miss Alderson are precisely the persons of whose society I am anxious to be quit ... I have come to the conclusion that I shall probably do Parliament well if I do marry and that I shall certainly make nothing of it if I do not ... I am exceedingly sorry that my adherence to this marriage should cause you such annoyance: but my conviction that I am right is too strong for me to give it up.*[1]

In July of 1857 he defiantly married Georgina at a small wedding, with the only attendant from the Cecils being his brave sister, Mildred, and her husband Alexander Beresford-Hope. His wife's family, further hurt by the death of Sir Edward, could only drum up an annual £100, leaving the couple to what Salisbury's father had threateningly called 'privations', struggling on £500 per annum in the relatively poky surrounds of the widowed mother-in-law's household.

The persons who will cut me because I marry Miss Alderson are precisely the persons of whose society I am anxious to be quit ...

SALISBURY

All things being relative, that sum was deemed to suffice for, say, 20 of the workers on the Hatfield estate, but the chasm between life at Hatfield House and in the Alderson house was very wide. It left the couple socially adrift, for there were snooty families who 'would not leave cards north of Oxford Street'. The newlyweds never visited the ancestral homestead until 1864.

The innermost secrets of the Victorian boudoir have

normally been preciously kept from the biographer's prying eye, the more so in a case like Lord Salisbury's, a man of unremitting reticence in private matters and who regarded the expression of private emotions as being indecent. The chaste passions of Charles and Mary Kingsley have been revealed to us, while Mary Penrose Arnold let slip how shaken she had been by the fierce demands of her husband, Thomas Arnold, but, these and other pieces of gossip apart, the 19th-century marital couch is alien territory. What is evident enough was that the newly-married couple went about their carnal duties with some heartiness and that Lord Salisbury was a more cheerful soul after than before his wedding night. With characteristically Victorian zeal, they had eight children, all born between 1858 and 1869. It would perhaps make sense to deal with this fecundity at one fell swoop, rather than to drip-feed each child separately into the narrative.

The first born was Maud, who arrived in 1858, and who later married the MP, Lord Selborne. Another daughter followed in 1860, this was Gwendolen, her father's adoring biographer. Then there was a run of three boys: James, born in 1861, the heir presumptive, who concentrated on the management of the estate and also had a political career; William, born in 1863, who went in the church and became, in 1889, the rector of Hatfield; and Robert, born in 1864, who took to the law by way of profession. Fanny, a third daughter, was born in 1866, but, sadly, she died 14 months later. Then came Edward in 1867, and he was bound for the army, while in 1869, there was another son, Hugh, who went into politics and became an MP. The way the boys contrived to spread themselves over the nap hand of careers open to the gentry is quite remarkable.

Assisted by the bright perceptions of his wife, Lord Salisbury, to his enormous credit, learnt the lessons of his horrid childhood and made strenuous efforts to ensure that his children were brought up in reasonable comfort, both physically and psychologically. He was a lenient and affectionate father, encouraging his youngsters to express themselves with a freedom unusual in Victorian family settings, with the result that the children appeared to have enjoyed friendly relations both with one another and with their parents, a total reverse of Lord Salisbury's own experience. His lack of restraint and formalism as a father also seems untypical of his generally buttoned-up demeanour in public life. One may imagine that he frequently returned to the solace of this contented nest, finding it restful after the buffets of political office and restorative of his energies for the next bout of political action. It forms one of the more pleasant images of Lord Salisbury's long life.

For all that, he was, in the interim, strapped for cash. Like the young Winston Churchill in similar straits, he turned resourcefully to journalism. From the time of his engagement to Georgina Alderson he wrote methodically and prodigiously to support his burgeoning household. He composed hundreds of lengthy articles and reviews, amounting, so diligent arithmetic research reports, to 1.5 million words between 1856 and 1866, principally for the right-wing journals, the weekly *Saturday Review* and the *Quarterly Review*. His writing was vigorous and opinionated, highly revealing of his traditionalist values but also showing his grasp of political realities. He was candid and sarcastic in his judgements, by his own lights honest and uncompromising, if, for the more compassionate reader, erring on the censorious side. Second in line to a great estate and beholden to no man except the Marquess of Exeter, with whom he was inevitably in accord, he was the servant of no master. He utilised this independence with assiduous rigour. Superficially, this sort of independence is attractive, but on the counter side, it meant that there were no checks and balances; Lord Salisbury was accountable to no one.

His style, lofty and weighty in the grand Victorian manner and spun out with learned reference, was very acceptable to his readership. Victorian culture was heavily literary in mode. When Queen Victoria ascended the throne, about 2,000 books were printed every year; by the time of her death it was 10,000. There were 42,000 Victorian novels, written by 3,500 Victorian novelists, and there was plenty of non-fiction, in book and journal form, as well as myriad newspapers, to complement that vast array. Many would have enjoyed the cutting edge of Lord Salisbury's magisterial and unsentimental assessments. In both speeches and articles, he constantly argued by telling analogue – he compared, for instance, General Sherman's destructive march through Georgia towards the end of the American Civil War with the barbaric exploits of Genghis Khan, while prostitutes in London were as overt as *fleas in an Italian bed*.[2] At times this could become heavy-handed, although on other occasions there was a waspish humour: his disgust with political processions and demonstrations was concisely demonstrated with his dismissive label, *legislation by picnic*.

He scribbled away ferociously for nine years – and then his ailing elder brother finally died in 1865. The family had gradually reconciled itself to the impecunious marriage and now, as heir, Lord Robert Gascoyne-Cecil was at last Viscount Cranborne. He took up his rightful place, financially and socially, and much of his journalistic activity, about which he would thereafter be very reticent, was ended.

Both in the House of Commons and in his industrious journalism, Lord Salisbury laid down a highly consistent political line. He supported the rebel Confederacy during the American Civil War and railed against the rampant demotic, industrialised power of the northern Union, to the point where he was unsympathetic to the assassination of President Lincoln in 1865. Conversely, the British union he regarded as inviolable and was unrepentant in his refusal to accede to Irish hopes of even the faintest of shifts towards self-determination.

He was fundamentally opposed to any reform of the parliamentary suffrage. A stout contender of the view that men acted always and narrowly out of self-interest, he believed that property and political power were rightly connected and that it was folly for the ruling class to proffer votes to the propertyless. The propertyless, he assumed, would deploy such newfound power to grab the property, whereas the propertied had the sense to keep the hordes at bay with sops, such as minimal poor relief. Complementary to this attitude was his view that there should be an Anglican primacy in government, and he was not keen to see parliament diluted by non-Anglicans – Roman Catholics, Jews, atheists and the like – so eager was he to protect the clerical component of the church-state constitution. In the same light, he worked hard to sustain the efforts of local Anglican church schools and contributed to the development of High Church boarding schools, such as Lancing and King Alfred's, Taunton.

During his early years in Parliament he was not offered office, in part because, during these confused political times, the Conservatives were not often able to form a stable administration, in part because he was not hesitant, in verbal or oral medium, in demonstrating his dislike of what he deemed to be the trickiness of his party leader, Benjamin Disraeli. However, when Lord Derby became Prime Minister for the third time in 1866, Lord Salisbury was offered the post of Secretary of State for India. He was appointed a Privy Councillor and entered the Cabinet, aged 36, having never had any previous experience in a junior office. It was also remunerative. Although, of course, MPs remained unpaid until just before the 1914–18 war, ministerial salaries were relatively high, and Lord Salisbury was paid an annual salary of £5,000. By way of comparison, Mrs Beeton's *Book of Household Management*, first published in 1861, contended that an income of a fifth of that, £1,000, could support a household with five servants, whilst the upper-middle class income bracket was judged as something between those two figures of £1,000 and £5,000.

The new minister's immediate and main preoccupation was with the Orissa famine in Eastern India, the cause of the death of a million people. An official understanding of the dangers of the catastrophe had been slow to emerge, but Lord Salisbury did make strenuous efforts to provide some amelioration of a ghastly situation. Since the Indian Mutiny of 1857/8 the authority of the East India Company had largely been superseded by a more direct governmental control. The old Board of Control had become the India Council, designed to give advice to the Secretary of State. For his part, Lord Salisbury took a typically unsentimental view of India and, like most of his contemporaries, believed that the balance of power was most effectively maintained by keeping the Indian princes in a condition of wary antagonism the one with another. It was not unlike his emergent view of how to deal with Europe.

His Cabinet office was short-lived. Disraeli, the keystone of the Derby administration, sought to seize the political initiative with an audacious plan to reform the parliamentary franchise, having stoutly led the assault on a recent Liberal attempt to pass a less radical measure. Since the repeal of the Corn Laws in 1846, and the subsequent split of the Conservative Party, national politics had been in something of a flux, with little continuity of governance and few chances for the Conservatives. Disraeli was naturally keen to restore the fortunes of his party and lead it forward in periods of sustained government.

His bold stroke was anathema to Lord Salisbury, who considered it a gross betrayal of the landed interest scarcely less heinous than that of Sir Robert Peel over the protection of home-produced corn, the very occasion of Disraeli's surfacing as prospective Tory leader. After much Cabinet manoeuvring, there were three resignations; as well as Lord Salisbury, Jonathan Peel, Sir Robert's brother, and Lord Carnarvon, a close associate of Salisbury, yielded up the seals of office. The 1867 Reform Act, in broad summary, gave the vote to the urban working man. At the consequent 1868 election 2.3 million votes were cast, as opposed to 855,000 at the preceding 1865 election. There were still 212 uncontested seats, including, inevitably, Stamford. Although the matter was not allowed to rest there, and agitation for the franchise for agricultural workers soon began, the collapse of society that Lord Salisbury had, in Cassandra mood, gloomily and blackly predicted, did not occur. As he began to perceive, there were ways and means of controlling the aftermath of reform.

In the interim, and bereft of his valued ministerial income, Lord Salisbury, never an expert economist, was further embarrassed by heavy losses, possibly over £20,000, in the Stock Exchange crisis of 1866, an experience that left him ever wary of the perils of unbridled capitalism. Rather reluctantly perhaps, he did what plenty of politicians, believing themselves to be impecunious, have done before and since. He took up the part-time post of executive chairman of the Great Eastern Railway, at an annual salary of £700. To be fair to Lord Salisbury, he was no seeker after sinecures, like some of the political breed, and, from 1868 to 1872, he introduced a sensible level of management to what had been an ailing enterprise.

He also turned to his father for financial aid but the outcome was sudden and dramatic. The Marquess died in 1868. Lord Salisbury found himself in the House of Lords and removed from what, by aristocratic standards, were cramped quarters to the opulent splendour of Hatfield House. Never again would he have either financial worries or any anxieties about the base of his political strength. The switch was as precipitous and colourful as a pantomime transformation scene. One of the curios of the hereditary principle is that one must anticipate the death of one's parent with some ambivalence. Lord Salisbury had mended a few filial fences of late but, all in all, his relationship with his father had been cool; at a stroke, the heir was one of the wealthiest men in Britain, with an estate valued at £300,000, the owner of 20,000 acres, spread over several shires, and a stately home, with more than a hundred rooms and the employer of some 250 servants and workers, plus urban estates in London and Liverpool. Although agricultural rents were subject to adjustment over the rest of the century, it is safe to assume that, henceforward, Lord Salisbury usually had a gross annual income of some £70,000 and a disposable annual income of over £50,000 – enough for 2,000 agricultural labourers. Moreover, in that distinctly hidebound hierarchical society, his immediate elevation to the House of Lords, with the exalted title of the 3rd Marquess of Salisbury, provided him with the ideal platform for the fulfilment of his political ambition. It may not have been quite Cinderella becoming the Princess Crystal, but his father's death was, in material and parliamentary terms, the makings of Lord Salisbury. His last speech in the Commons was, characteristically enough, a tirade against Gladstone's move to disestablish the Irish church. Thereafter he more or less turned his back on the lower and concentrated his attention on the upper house, intent not only in using it for his own personal power base but in strengthening its ability to defend his nation and his class against radical onslaught.

Lord Salisbury, that title now safely his, took his seat in the Lords on the eve of the 1868 general election which resulted in a decisive Liberal victory and a reforming Gladstonian administration. This gave the new Marquess some time to spend in and around his estate, where he proved to be a concerned if paternalistic landlord. His knowledgeable interest in technical matters is illustrated by his installation of electric lighting at Hatfield House in 1874, seven years, for instance, before Richard D'Oyly Carte's Savoy became the first London theatre to be so illuminated. He involved himself with practical issues, like cottage building, the inevitable new church school, water supply and a post office and he generally improved the local habitat. The Cecil's town house in Arlington Street, rebuilt at the enormous cost of £60,000, in the fashionable St James' district of London, became an important bastion of Lord Salisbury's political and allied social activity. As many as a thousand could be entertained there and it was often to be utilised for major political meetings, with Lady Salisbury very much in her element as both the town and country hostess. There were other than political gatherings. A frequent guest at both sites was Charles Lutwidge Dodgson, better known as Lewis Carroll. There cannot have been a more distinguished celebrant of the 'discovery of childhood,' invited to entertain noble offspring. Lord Salisbury's sons received £1,000 a year from their kindly father when they reached adulthood.

The Salisburys also had a holiday home near Dieppe, no simple villa this but, as photographs suggest, a building that resembled the mock-Gothic town hall of a Victorian provincial city. Later they created a holiday haunt at Beaulieu on the French Riviera. In 1869 Lord Salisbury was also made Chancellor of Oxford University, another responsibility he took with due seriousness as defender of its ancient rights. If his political party were the natural fold for supporters of the Anglican primacy, then Oxford was the complementary training school. The solemnly religious Lewis Carroll was a don at Christ Church, Oxford and had become known to Lord Salisbury through his chancellorship.

Lord Salisbury is a notable example of the way in which the so-called 'charmed circle', the manner in which the landed aristocracy contrived to retain much political power after its economic potency had waned, had some very pragmatic aspects. One was the momentum of an early start to a parliamentary career. With safer seats and often without the distractions of other professional calls on their time, the young noblemen were able to enjoy something like an administrative apprenticeship. Several, like Lord Salisbury, were prepared to work with diligent industry and do less glamorous jobs, such as the Secretaryship of India. All this enabled some of them to make a reasonable cockshy at being ministers and thus the landed interest tended to be over represented in the councils of the nation.

The one blot on the Cecil family escutcheon at this time was the marriage of Lord Salisbury's stepmother, Mary Sackville-West, to Lord Derby in 1870. The previous Lord Derby, who had been Prime Minister and leader of the Conservative Party, had died in 1869, and this was his son, hitherto known as Lord Stanley. Lord Salisbury's relations with the new groom were decidedly uneasy, despite their common political and social affiliations. The reasons for their feuding are obscure. There were some differences of political opinion, for Lord

Stanley was, in Salisbury's outspoken view, lax on some issues, while there were rumours that, first, Lord Stanley had been Georgina Alderson's first choice of a husband before, on his indifference, she turned her attentions more effectively in Lord Salisbury's direction; and, second, that Stanley had had an affair with his future bride while the 2nd Marquess of Salisbury was still in the land of the living. It must also have irked Lord Salisbury that he was obliged to pay a huge annuity – £5,000 a year – to his stepmother, even though her second husband, now the Earl of Derby, had estates almost four times the size of Hatfield.

Throughout the Liberal ministry of 1868 to 1874 Lord Salisbury sustained his anti-reformist stance. He opposed the 1872 Secret Ballot Act, on the somewhat specious grounds that it would dissuade the respectable members of the community from voting; he opposed the Irish Land Act, which sought to control rents, on the customary grounds that it was an infringement of the rights of contract; he opposed the 1871 Army Regulation Act, aimed at the abolition of purchased commissions, on the doubtful grounds that it would lead to 'jobbery' and corrupt practice. Lord Salisbury also developed a shrewd line in opposition; he advised his fellow peers not to vote against the bill to disestablish the Irish church, something he totally disagreed with, because that proposal had figured strongly in the Liberal election manifesto. He underlined the corollary; namely, a warning that anything that did not have such a mandate could be severely attacked.

The Conservatives won the 1874 election. A tired Liberal Party, wearied by busy sessions of reforming legislation on issues that ranged from education and licensing to the civil service and trades unions, and worn down by the problems of Ireland, was defeated. The Conservatives totalled 350 seats, against the Liberal tally of 242, with 60 seats going to the Irish Nationalists. Lord Salisbury was faced with a personal dilemma. His ambition was not excessive. He believed he had some obligation to serve to the best of his ability and by the lights of his political creed and he had some powerful desire so to do. Having consciously picked the political road, it was, to him, foolhardy to choose to be a passenger and not a driver. His problem was with Disraeli, the new Prime Minister, for he was a politician whom Lord Salisbury both disliked and distrusted. Nor had he been less than forthright in his trenchant criticism of the leader of the party. However, after a few wobbles and some indeterminate manoeuvrings, he agreed to take on the role of Secretary of State for India once more.

Just as his first stint at the India office had been marked by the Orissa famine, now there was further famine in Bengal, and Lord Salisbury tried to deal with this expedi-

Benjamin Disraeli, Earl of Beaconsfield (1804–81) played a leading part in the foundation of the modern Conservative Party. Entering Parliament in 1837, he first rose to prominence by attacking the repeal of the Corn Laws. Twice Chancellor of the Exchequer, he first became Prime Minister in 1868, his second term lasting from 1874 to 1880. His 1867 Reform Act greatly widened the franchise, and his second premiership saw the acquisition of the Suez Canal, Queen Victoria becoming Empress of India, and his personal triumph at the Congress of Berlin in 1878.

ently, raising loans and endeavouring to establish irrigation schemes. He supervised the plans for the Prince of Wales' visit to the sub-continent in 1875, attempted to find some balance of Lancashire and Indian interests on the vexed question of cotton duties and kept a beady eye on any signs of encroaching Russian influence on India. He was characteristically unimpressed by Disraeli's flamboyant gesture of 1876 in granting Queen Victoria's urgent wish to become Empress of India. It seemed rather un-English to Salisbury.

He also became embroiled at home with Disraeli over the Public Worship Regulation Bill, a measure, much admired by Queen Victoria, to outlaw 'Romish practices' in the Church of England. Lord Salisbury thought this would cause strife among the clergy and be counterproductive. It looked as if his second Cabinet office would be as short-lived as his first. Disraeli launched a furious assault on him, saying: 'He is not a man who measures his phrases. He is a great master of jibes and flouts and jeers, but I do not suppose there is anyone who is prejudiced against a Member of Parliament on account of such qualifications.'[3] As sometimes happens with such exchanges, Disraeli's outburst, after years of silence in the face of Salisburyan assaults, cleared the air and the relationship between the two men improved. It was as well, for they were to share in a major crisis that brought credit to both their reputations and which was to precipitate Lord Salisbury to the forefront of European diplomacy.

'He is a great master of jibes and flouts and jeers …'

DISRAELI ON SALISBURY

This concern arose from the complex Eastern Question. Disraeli had resolved to adopt a grandiloquent tone in foreign affairs, as a direct converse of Gladstone's moralistic approach of what he called 'public right'. Soon after Disraeli had formed his administration, there were troubles in the Ottoman Empire, based on Constantinople. This was an ailing enterprise, on the verge of bankruptcy, and some of its constituent parts, among them Bosnia and Herzegovina, showed evident signs of unrest. Russia and Austria suggested various reforms and concessions as a solution, about which Disraeli blew hot and cold.

With France weakened by defeat in the Franco-Prussian War of 1870/1, Russia was regarded as the prime menace to English interests. The newly-unified states of Germany and Austria were virtually landlocked and neither was, at that stage, a colonial rival. On the other hand, Russia, through control of Constantinople and the Straits, might have gained influence in the Mediterranean and threatened the short route to India, especially after Disraeli's coup in 1875 of purchasing the Suez Canal. There was also the rather more remote fear of Russian penetration, military or commercial, into Afghanistan and hence into Asia proper.

Thus for defensive reasons Disraeli was keen to bolster the tottering Turkish regime. He was embarrassed by the ferocity of the Turkish response to insurgency, when the irregular Bashi-Bazouk troops committed atrocities against the largely Christian populations of the rebellious provinces. Gladstone campaigned vigorously up and down the country, arousing great anger about the treatment of the Christian minorities and urging that the Turks should be ousted, 'bag and baggage', from the Bulgarian territory they had 'profaned'. This crusade, part a cry for self-determination, part an appeal on grounds of religious persecution, attracted enormous national support. Gladstone equated what he called 'Beaconfieldism' (Disraeli was made Earl of Beaconsfield in 1876) with cynical opportunism. This was, considering the relative remoteness of the Balkan outrages, one of the most spectacularly successful extra-parliamentary agitations of the century.

Disraeli was saved by the over-confidence of both the Russians and the Turks. The latter thought that they could hold their own against Russia and that, in the last resort, Britain would come to their aid. A cocksure but financially weak Russia declared war on Turkey in 1877 and, after some unexpected and draining setbacks, imposed on the Turks the 1878 Treaty of San Stefano. England had a fleet already anchored outside the Dardanelles and it sailed towards Constantinople, while Indian troops were ostentatiously moved to Malta. There were vivid signs of war fever in Britain. This is the moment when the Great McDermott, appearing at the London Pavilion music hall, gave vent to the ditty:

'We don't want to fight, but, by jingo, if we do,
We've got the men, we've got the ships; we've got the
   money, too.'

This original excursion into 'Jingoism' was ephemeral enough. Austria and Prussia were as alarmed as Britain at the Russian advances and plans were discussed to halt them. It was here that Lord Salisbury came into his own as a superior diplomat. He had already visited the key capitals as a senior kind of envoy figure – Constantinople, Berlin, Vienna, Rome – in a gruelling series of encounters with the leading players, including Bismarck. He had insisted both that the Turks should accept constitutional reforms in their possessions and that Russia should not become too embroiled in these affairs.

Although his tour did not immediately furnish positive results, he had made himself well known to the European chancelleries. More important still was the resignation from the Foreign Office of Lord Derby, something of an isolationist in European matters and whose wife, Salisbury's stepmother, was suspected of conducting a two-way exchange of information with Russian diplomats. Lord Salisbury was appointed Foreign Secretary. It might be said that, from that moment, he controlled the foreign policy of the nation until near the time of his death.

He acted with swift dispatch. He drafted the 'Salisbury Circular' that was distributed to the major European powers, among them Germany, where Bismarck was eager to play 'the honest broker' in a dispute that had few frissons for the new German nation-state. The Russians had insisted on a huge indemnity from the Ottoman Empire, on the creation of a 'Big Bulgaria' as a major bulwark against the Turks and on independence for Romania, Montenegro and Serbia. As far as the Conservative Cabinet was concerned, this adversely affected the pro-British balance in the Mediterranean. The Treaty of Berlin in 1878 reversed enough of this to please the British and much of the 'Salisbury Circular' was agreed.

The partition or dismemberment of the Turkish empire in Europe was put on hold; the 'Big Bulgaria' was trisected; Bosnia and Herzegovina were placed in Austrian hands; and, in compensation for some minor Russian gains in the Caucasus, Britain obtained the useful base of Cyprus, ideal for keeping a watch both on Russia and Turkey. Disraeli and Salisbury had toiled cooperatively together, the one the maestro of the public conduct of the debates, the other the dedicated master of the essential detail, rather like the best kind of rapport one might hope for in the head and deputy head of a thriving school.

The duo returned home in triumph, very much enjoyed by the Prime Minister, with his claim of 'peace, I hope,

Otto von Bismarck (1815–98) was the creator of a united Germany and dominated European diplomacy for 30 years. Appointed Prime Minister of Prussia in 1862, war with Denmark in 1864, with Austria in 1866 and France in 1870–1, in a policy of 'Blood and Iron', created the German Empire with Prussia as the dominant force within it. After the coronation of Kaiser Wilhelm I, Bismarck, now Imperial Chancellor, worked to preserve the Empire through diplomacy and a careful balance of power. He was dismissed in 1890 by Kaiser Wilhelm II, who wished to rule alone.

with honour', and less so by the undemonstrative Foreign Secretary, who diffidently accepted the Order of the Garter for his considerable pains – or, as the wits mocked, 'peace with honours'. Although Gladstone was suitably unimpressed, his acute colleague and biographer, John Morley, concluded that the Treaty of Berlin was a splendid ratification of Gladstonian policy. Be that as it may, it gave Lord Salisbury enormous standing in the Conservative Party in Parliament and in the country and was the foundation of his successful bid for the leadership of the party a few years later. Of incidental interest in the context of this biographical series is the fact that it was in the formulation of the actual treaty of Berlin that the title 'Prime Minister' was first officially used.

There were some other problems for the new Foreign Secretary, mostly connected with imperial possessions. There were the Afghan Wars, created by the undue zeal of the Viceroy of India, Lord Lytton, in pre-empting Russian advances in Afghanistan. This rather unnecessarily led to two campaigns, led by Major General Roberts, around the Afghan capital, Kabul. In South Africa it was, again, reckless behaviour by the local incumbent, Sir Bartle Frere, the High Commissioner, which led to trouble. The British found themselves fighting the redoubtable Zulus. They suffered a humbling defeat at Isandhlwana early in 1879, from which carnage some prestige was salvaged by the successful defence later the same day of B Company of the 24th (2nd Warwicks) Regiment of Foot at the cinematic location of Rorke's Drift. Eleven VCs were awarded to those heroes, masking, sceptics thought (for political spin is not a novel device) the other dreadful news. A punitive victory at the battle of Ulundi restored imperial nerves, but South Africa was to prove a major testing-ground for colonial policy before the century's end.

These two examples of the home government having

to move hurriedly to save face after impromptu and head-strong localised decisions remind us that neither Disraeli nor Lord Salisbury were so lustful of imperial conquest for its own sake as Gladstone, in his famous anti-imperialist Mid-lothian campaign of that time, and later critics have main-tained. In particular, Lord Salisbury preferred to judge case by case, rather than to have an open policy of aggrandise-ment, and he did not always like Disraeli's astute but never too costly playing of the imperial card as a political gambit. Nonetheless, Lord Salisbury accepted that there was an inner dynamism at work and that it was, he felt, perilous to rest on one's laurels and allow other nations to gain ground. In his imperialist as in much of his other political thinking, Salisbury was a practitioner, not an ideologue.

Lord Salisbury was indeed an astute observer of the global scene. The Paris Commune of 1870, with its inherent message that the ardent rebelliousness of 1789 had not been extin-guished, had shaken him. He would always be conscious, perhaps over-conscious, of this revolutionary danger. One of his worries about the United States was its love of demotic glories. With one eye on the vulnerability of Canada to American avarice, he would have preferred a split union, *nicely divided into two hostile states*.[4] It is a paradox, as com-mentators such as Gore Vidal have pointed out, that the great Abraham Lincoln created, by his stupendous and humane efforts, a centralised superstate that has not always, in the views of its several critics, abided by his civilised principles. Lord Salisbury constantly overestimated the, for him, dire effects of purported democracy. He forever anticipated that unalloyed democracy would be *a steamroller*, demolishing all traditional order. At best, it has proved, from that standpoint, little more than a lawn mower.

Nevertheless, he was prescient about such matters. He

believed in the 1870s that there were only three great powers – the United States, who could put a federal army of two million in the field; Russia, weighing in with an army of two million, and Germany with a military strength of over 1.5 million men. Against this the small British army and a navy that, obviously, could not be deployed in every conceivable campaign, was of little basic worth, while France was of no account. He even considered a conscription scheme, with the characteristic rider that richer draftees could pay substitutes to replace them. He regarded British 'greatness' as an illusion that could only be preserved by clever diplomacy. It was for this reason that he usually sought, as with the Turkish question, a working but never over-formalised arrangement with Germany. As in that Russo-Turkish crisis of 1876 and in later emergencies, he strove to avoid a war by, as he slyly said, demonstrating the will *to prepare for one ostentatiously*.[5] It was a cliff-hanging stratagem he played very coolly.

1880 saw the end of the Disraeli government, berated, especially in respect of foreign adventures, by the Gladstonian Liberals. Ceaseless work in office had damaged the health, rarely first-rate, of Lord Salisbury and he was struck violently ill with kidney disease. He was unable to take any part in the general election of that year, a contest that the Liberals comfortably won. The figures reversed those of 1874: 352

William Ewart Gladstone (1809–98) was the outstanding Liberal statesman of the 19th century. Originally a Tory, he had split from his party over the Corn Laws, and became a Liberal in 1859. Leader of the party from 1866, he was Prime Minister four times (1868–74, 1880–5, 1886 and 1892–4). His third term saw the British intervention in Egypt and the Sudan, while his later career was dominated by the issue of home rule for Ireland, which split the Liberal Party in 1886.

Liberals; 237 Tories and 63 Irish Nationalists. Always a little over the top in his gloomy prognostications, Lord Salisbury earnestly believed that this election heralded the declaration of the class war, but it introduced little more than a messy series of skirmishes about Ireland, Egypt, parliamentary reform and a few other topics.

Benjamin Disraeli, the Earl of Beaconsfield, did not long survive this defeat; he died in 1881. There followed a dual leadership of the Conservative Party, with Sir Stafford Northcote, previously Disraeli's Chancellor of the Exchequer, in the Commons and Lord Salisbury in the Lords. An intriguing thread, woven through the ensuing four or five years, was the discreet competition to reduce the twosome to one prior to the next general election. In hindsight, one may assess that Northcote was always likely to be unsuccessful. Faced with Gladstone in the Commons and by no means the most charismatic of politicians, the odds were stacked against him. Lord Salisbury lorded it over the Lords, aided by the fact that so many of the subjects under discussion were – Ireland is a prime example – non-domestic, thereby feeding his strengths.

Lord Salisbury was now 50 years old. For all but the last year or so of his life, Lord Salisbury would henceforward be the nominal or titular leader of the Conservative Party and for much the greater part of that period he would be Prime Minister. Having considered his life to that point, it is legitimate to merge together, for the central portion of this book, descriptions of the rest of his life and of his work as Prime Minister.

Lord Salisbury would from now until the end of the century, and even allowing for the continued endeavours of an ageing William Gladstone, dominate the British political landscape.

Part Two

THE LEADERSHIP

Chapter 3: Towards the Premiership

The 20 or so years of Lord Salisbury's predominance saw Britain's population rise from 35 million in 1881 to 42 million in 1901. This was a slackening of the demographic pace from the early decades of the century that owed something to the decrease in the birth rate from 36 to 29 per thousand of the population. The social mood and cultural climate began to favour what was known as 'the limited family'. It was in the 1880s that the term 'contraception', shyly and in veiled phrases, first entered public discourse, some of it self-defeating, as medical opinion then placed the time of safety in the menstrual cycle at exactly the moment of greatest risk. Later and fewer marriages was another factor in curtailing family size.

The demographic picture was also affected by an improved death rate, down over this 20-year period from 21 to 17 per thousand, chiefly as diseases like tuberculosis came more under control. Another reason was emigration – an average of well over 200,000 people left the country every year, the majority, interestingly enough, going to the USA. Nonetheless, the crucial backdrop was the gloom that hung over the economy in these years, for, as the developing industrial nations emulated the pioneer work of Britain, exports slowed and imports quickened. It was a complicated picture. The agricultural depression was evident enough. Arable farming suffered, to the tune of something like two-thirds of lost acreage, from the purchase of cheap American grains, whilst pastoral farming lost out to the importation of refrigerated meat. In industry, however, there were losses and gains, with, by way of example, textiles and steel suffering setbacks but shipbuilding and, among newer enterprises, bicycle manufactures flourishing. Although unemployment rose from the 1 per cent of the peak boom year of 1872 to over 10 per cent in the bad years of the last two decades of the century, the real value of wages increased by something like 40 per cent. Moreover, there was a constant fillip for the economy in the rising value of invisible earnings, principally to do with financial services, like insurance, banking and overseas investment.

When Lord Salisbury was born more than half the population lived in the countryside. When he died the majority, 77 per cent, lived in towns, that is, in communities of 5,000 or more and over half of those urban residents were located in cities of more than 100,000 inhabitants – the town planner, Patrick Geddes, coined the descriptive word 'conurbation' in 1915. In roughly approximate fractions, the working classes outnumbered the upper and middle classes by 78 per cent to 22 per cent, the latter figure recently swollen by burgeoning numbers in commerce and the professions.

An aspect of this, and one that Lord Salisbury and his colleagues would take seriously from a party-political stance, was the growth of suburbia. For instance, the suburban outer fringes of London more than doubled in the 20 years of Salisbury's overlordship. The quintessential text of suburban existence – George and Weedon Grossmith's *Diary of a Nobody* – was published in 1892 and its anti-hero, Mr Pooter, a denizen of Holloway, represented fictitiously those adherents to 'Villa Toryism' whom the Conservative party managers would soon have in their sights.

So much for the chief social facts in regard of British life in the last two decades of the 19th century. They were peaceful enough years, both at home, where the crime rate dipped encouragingly, and, imperial excursions always excepted, abroad. Many British people enjoyed a reasonable standard of living. They were, however, sobering years compared with the excitements of mid-century, when British industry had been unrivalled and her foreign policies pugnaciously outgoing. The mood, some of it expressed in the *fin de siècle* art and writing of the 1890s, was a little less buoyant than earlier in the Victorian period. In Lord Salisbury, pessimistic, minimalist, wary, the era found an appropriate spokesman.

We regard it [change] *as an evil, and we do not desire to give it any assistance we can avoid.*

SALISBURY

Parliament is a potent engine and its enactments must always do something, but they very seldom do what the originators of these enactments meant.[1] Ever suspicious of change, Lord Salisbury also declared that, although it was sometimes impossible to dodge*, we regard it as an evil, and we do not desire to give it any assistance we can avoid.*[2]

Gladstone's second administration, never the equal of his first ministry in respect of positive domestic reforms, rather played into Lord Salisbury's capable hands by its concentration on the seemingly insoluble Irish problem and on tricky imperial matters. Lord Salisbury vehemently opposed Gladstone's attempts to conciliate the militant Irish tenants by land reforms, all of which were regarded by the Conservative leader as infringements of the law of contract. He accused the *ignorant peasantry* in Ireland of *shooting people to whom they owed money.* The Liberals urged the acceptance of 'the Three F's' – fair rents, fixity of tenure and free sale – in their Irish Land Bill of 1881, a measure Lord Salisbury fought all the way in the House of Lords, causing anxiety among his less forthright colleagues as well as chagrin on the government benches. As ever, he was keen to promote the potency of the Lords, arguing that the Liberals had strayed beyond their mandate.

The atmosphere was radically changed, first, by the release in 1882 of Charles Parnell from Kilmainham gaol, where the Irish Nationalist leader had been interned as part of the government's coercive policy to crack down on violence in Ireland. He had apparently agreed to use his influence to terminate the 'land war', but then, second, by the dreadful news of the Phoenix Park murders, the double assassination of Lord Frederick Cavendish, the newly appointed Chief Secretary for Ireland and Gladstone's nephew-in-law, and T H Burke, the hated Irish Under-secretary. The government was in some disarray, but Lord Salisbury did overreach himself rather, later in 1882. He proved to be more uncompromising than his fellow Tory peers could stomach over Gladstone's Irish rent arrears legislation, whereby the state would subsidise the payment of rents where poverty could be properly demonstrated. Few Tories wished to risk the election that Gladstone threatened, whilst Irish landlords, less wedded than Lord Salisbury to purity of contract, were not too fussy about whence their money emanated. This was a slight setback for Lord Salisbury, normally much more sure-footed on such procedural matters, but, an astute learner from error, he rarely again missed his constitutional footing. Moreover, in the mid-term, his bristling intransigence impressed his colleagues.

The Liberal government never quite recovered its equilibrium and, in 1884, when Gladstone brought forward his bill to put the rural workers on the same electoral level as urban workers, Lord Salisbury played an astute hand. In what was a rough campaign, he again evoked the spectre of a Lords veto, hopeful that the measure would fall. When this proved not to be the case, he requested the quid pro quo of redistribution. His pragmatic view was that, without some redistribution of seats, the Conservative Party was faced with longstanding under-representation. Using the central motif of single-member constituencies, he negotiated, in a confidential agreement known as the Arlington Street Compact, a satisfactory compromise.

The 1884/85 Parliamentary Reform Act (Representation of the People Act and Redistribution of Seats Act) notionally added over two million voters to the existing three million on the registers, but the more dramatic change was the shift to 670 constituencies of roughly equal populations, the huge majority of them with single members, not two as in the past. The 79 boroughs of less than 15,000 inhabitants were absorbed into the nearest county district; boroughs with 50,000 to 165,000 did retain two members, whilst those with more than 165,000 were divided into single divisions. The upshot was that the Liberals were incommoded in towns where they had carefully fielded a 'Whig' and a 'Radical' candidate and collected both seats, while, in that the new divisions frequently followed the lines of social class housing, Conservative votes were successfully corralled. Importantly, patches of freshly minted suburbia on the fringes of towns were incorporated into county constituencies, matching the new rural labouring voters, some of whom were keen to thwart the Tory squire and parson. Lord Salisbury was thus able to utilise a quite rational redistribution of voters to enhance the Conservative interest.

Gladstone, never as nimble as Salisbury as a reader of either electoral or imperial events, was further embarrassed by the machinations of the vain, disobedient General Gordon who died his perhaps yearned for martyr's death at the siege of Khartoum in 1885. Gladstone soon resigned on a marginal issue and, prior to the general election that would follow when the new boundary changes and registers were completed, Queen Victoria, spurning the hopes of Sir Stafford Northcote, the long-time favourite, asked Lord Salisbury to form a government. She now believed him to be the best anti-Gladstone candidate with an outside chance of saving her from more years of trial at the hands of her least favourite premier. After some demur over minor technical issues about sustaining the actual sinews of governance, he agreed so to do.

Thus Lord Salisbury formed his first administration, which lasted five months from the summer of 1885 to the general election in November. In that contest the Conservatives did lose some 'agricultural' seats but not as many as might have been anticipated. Apart from Lord Salisbury's shrewd redistribution schedule, there were also voters in the towns attracted by the Tory Party's opposition to expensive radical Liberal plans and by the first sightings of a 'fair trade', that is, mildly protectionist, policy as opposed to the Liberal free trade policy.

In the event, the Liberals won 344 to the Conservatives' 249 seats, with the Irish Nationalists holding the balance with a strong minority of 85 MPs. Within months the Liberal Party was irretrievably split by Gladstone's pursuit of Home Rule for Ireland. Having held the ascendancy for much of the time since the 1830s, a dominance aided by the fission of the Tories at the time of Sir Robert Peel's abolition of the Corn Laws in 1846, the Whigs/Liberals were torn asunder. They would not regain genuine command – and then only briefly – until the Edwardian period.

Another election followed in 1886. This time the Conservatives, with Lord Salisbury the accepted leader, won 316 seats, while they formed what was sometimes called a 'virtual coalition' with the 77 Liberal dissident 'Unionists', that is, defenders of Irish inclusion within the British ambit. Lord Salisbury formed his second administration, one that endured until 1892, exactly six years, then the normal term. He had a working majority of around 60.

The Liberals narrowly won the 1892 general election, as the Liberal Unionists were reduced from 77 to 46. The Liberals now fielded 273 MPs, which, together with 81 Irish Home Rulers, gave them a not very stable majority of about 40 over the 'virtual coalition' of 269 Tories and 46 Unionists. The 1893 Home Rule Bill, a much more substantial proposal than its predecessor of 1886, was thrown out by Lord Salisbury and his fellows in the House of Lords, and Gladstone resigned his fourth premiership. The mercurial and insomniac Lord Rosebery, whose horse, Ladas, won the 1894 Derby, replaced him, almost purely on Queen Victoria's say-so. The Derby triumph proved to be just about his sole success, as his administration, hounded constantly by the upper house, soon collapsed.

The Conservatives won the subsequent election easily. With their 340 seats and the Liberal Unionists' 71, a total of 411 outnumbered the struggling Liberals, on 177, plus 82 Irish Nationalists, by a majority of 152. With the Conservative and Unionist alliance growing ever closer, Lord Salisbury was in a robust position as he chose his third ministry, one that lasted from the summer of 1895 to the summer of 1902.

This seven-year phase included a further electoral success for Lord Salisbury in the so-called 'Khaki Election' of October 1900, a barefaced exploitation of the emotional mood consequent on delayed but eventual martial success in the Boer War. Despite the government's problems at this stage, Lord Salisbury was able to prolong his premiership with much the same majority – about 130 – that, following a series of by-election defeats, he had enjoyed just prior to that contest. The election date was carefully chosen. Further buffeted by internal arguments about the Boer War, the Liberals had not yet recovered anything like their old equilibrium and 149 seats – more than even the 117 of 1895 – went unopposed, most of them falling to the Conservatives. Those 149 constituencies represented 35 per cent of the electorate.

Such, in brief outline, is the pattern of Lord Salisbury's authority during the last years of the 19th and the opening months of the 20th centuries. All in all, he was Prime Minister for thirteen and a half years, out of a possible 16 years. It makes for a remarkably compact, as well as an exceptionally long, period of overall control of a nation's destinies. During this time the chief elements of political discourse tended, not unnaturally, to remain the same. The questions of Ireland, of Africa, of Europe, as well as certain domestic topics, like education, housing and local government, were always on the political agenda. For this reason, and also to undertake an analysis of Lord Salisbury in all his facets as a premier, it might be expedient to examine this intensely busy political era thematically rather than chronologically.

Three headings will be used. The first will introduce a look at Lord Salisbury in his own preferred role as master of overseas affairs, touching on his undoubted influence on European, imperial and – because he himself viewed the subject in this European and imperial context – Ireland. The second will turn to Lord Salisbury's domestic record, itself of course affected for good and ill by events abroad. An attempt will be made to assess Lord Salisbury's continued endeavour, in particular, to protect the landed interest and the role of the Established Church and, in general, to moderate the pace of what he believed to be a destabilising 'progress'. The third will scrutinise Lord Salisbury's ability as a political leader, for, in a period of political flux, he showed a fascinating talent – as his part in the redistribution discussions of 1884/5 has already revealed – in engineering Conservative efficacy across a range of political agencies from the House of Lords to local government.

Chapter 4: Lord Salisbury Abroad

When they [the other European powers] *find out what our policy really is, that we are there merely to extend to others the blessings we ourselves enjoy; when they find that we welcome their competition, that we invite every trade, that we grudge success to no nationality ... then I believe all idea of jealousy will vanish and that they will heartily cooperate with us in our civilising mission.*[1]

Apart from the first five months of his second ministry, during which Sir Stafford Northcote, now Lord Iddesleigh, held the office, and the last 20 months of his third administration, when Lord Lansdowne took over, Lord Salisbury was always his own Foreign Secretary. He maintained the view that a Prime Minister *has no powers*, especially if he were in the House of Lords. The Prime Minister, for Lord Salisbury, was rather like Thomas Hardy's 'president of the immortals', watching over a process he had set in motion but with which he preferred not to interfere. Even when he grudgingly yielded up the seals of the Foreign Secretaryship, he became Lord Privy Seal, insisting that he must hold some governmental post. Of course, most prime ministers more or less willingly become engaged in global affairs and Lord Salisbury did have the perfect excuse that he was more knowledgeable about such matters than any other of his colleagues. Building on the respect he had commanded among foreign powers since his negotiations at the time of the Treaty of Berlin in 1878, his confident and lengthy authority grew proportionately over the years.

There is little doubt that, despite the strain on his health, he enjoyed the minutiae of diplomatic entanglement more than any other aspect of government. His biographer, Michael Bentley, has written of his 'chess-playing mentality' in such matters and this is a telling metaphor, for he showed great ingenuity in foreseeing the second and third phase effects of each move. Perhaps the analogy of the snooker player would be even more precise, relevantly enough, with snooker being a game devised in the Raj at the Devonshire Regiment's officers' mess in Jubulpore in 1875 by an officer named Neville Chamberlain – not, of course, the future premier, who was only six at the time. Lord Salisbury, having played a diplomatic shot, appeared to know exactly where all the balls, particularly the white ball of England, would be located when they all came to a halt. Britain became near to being governed by an expert diplomatist rather than an all-round politician.

He deemed this to be the all-encompassing purpose of government. He took very seriously the concept of what has been called the 'night watchman' state, casting himself in that very role of ensuring that the busy streets were satisfactorily patrolled while the British (or rather, in his mind, 'English') household was permitted to go about its lawful occasions without let or hindrance. One consequence of his running of the nation from Horse Guards Parade rather than Downing Street, and his nurture of and closeness to a strong network of overseas ambassadors and the like, was an ascendancy of the Foreign Office for decades in the counsels of the nation, an ascendancy reassumed by 'the Gladstonian garrison' of the Treasury (much disliked by Lord Salisbury) after 1945.

Throughout these years his main priority was to sustain an informal friendship with Germany. Germany entered into the forceful partnership of the Triple Alliance with Austria-Hungary and Italy by 1882, with Bismarck the arch exponent of an adroit scheme to check Russian and French ambition. France and Russia formed their own defensive alliance in 1894. It benefited Germany to encourage cleavage between Britain and Germany's neighbours to west and east, and, on the whole, Lord Salisbury was complacent about this.

In 1882, Gladstone ordered military intervention in Egypt after a revolt by army officers threatened British interests in the Suez Canal, the fleet bombarding Alexandria and Sir Garnet Wolseley defeating the rebel army at Tel El Kebir. British involvement escalated as they were drawn into fighting the Madhist uprising in the Sudan, and the death of General Gordon at Khartoum in 1885 helped bring down Gladstone's government. In 1898, the British under Kitchener avenged Gordon at the Battle of Omdurman, defeating the Khalifa's forces and bringing all of the Sudan under British control.

An example of the former attitude — the continuous friction with France — concerned the unauthorised occupation of Egypt, consequent on its invasion in 1882, under the orders of the then Liberal administration, in which, in a most effective operation, Sir Garnet Wolseley had restored calm and embedded British influence. This had had the effect of obscuring the long-standing joint influence of France in the area. Lord Salisbury inherited this situation, whereby Turkey was the nominal suzerain but Britain the real regulator of Egypt.

Bismarck was content with this situation, especially as joint financial guarantees of large loans to that country by the European powers left Britain heavily reliant on German goodwill. Similarly Bismarck had helped engineer, to the annoyance of the French, the 1881 Italian occupation of Tunis, which, in turn, appealed to Britain, fearful otherwise of a French grip on the western Mediterranean. Lord Salisbury, cleverly exploiting the anomalous position of Turkey and with the benign support of Germany, maintained the position, aided by the work of Sir Evelyn Baring as agent and consul-general in Cairo for a long and influential spell. It would be the 1950s before this arrangement was ended by the departure of British troops from Egypt.

An example of the latter – the Russian – aspect of compliance with the Triple Alliance was in 1885, when there was a minor replay of the 'Big Bulgaria' problem of the 1870s. Eastern Rumelia tried to reunite with Bulgaria, but, such were the machinations of Balkan politics, Russia opposed the move, as Bulgaria now had an anti-Russian government. Tiny Serbia, seeking some addition to its own territory, invaded Bulgaria but was so soundly repulsed that Austria-Hungary stepped in to protect the vanquished Serbs, increasingly vulnerable to Russian depredations.

Lord Salisbury now believed again in his old view that propping up the Turks was a wasteful policy; stronger Balkan states, such as a tough Bulgaria, might prove a more efficient means of checking Russian designs on the Near East. Thus he colluded with Austria-Hungary and Germany in an anti-Russian 'bigger' Bulgaria and its unity around a new monarch, Ferdinand of Saxe-Coburg, usefully a relative by marriage of Queen Victoria. There was also some further resolution through an exchange of notes in 1887, known as the Mediterranean Agreements, whereby several of the powers pledged to prevent the predominance of any other great power in and around the Mediterranean. This, too, was aimed especially against Russia and France.

Gladstone was, on the whole, in agreement with this procedure, just as Lord Salisbury, rather more unwillingly, had felt obliged to acquiesce in Gladstone's Egyptian occupation. Here was the base for something of a cross-party consensus on foreign affairs that endured for several years. It is worth recalling that the 1839 British guarantee of Belgian independence, the immediate and overt reason for British entry into the First World War in 1914, had been primarily directed against France. When there were fears of a Franco-German war in 1887/8, prompted by fresh French designs on the always disputed lands of Alsace-Lorraine, Lord Salisbury allowed heavy hints to be dropped about the application of that guarantee in favour of a friendly Germany. The measures taken at this time by Lord Salisbury's government to protect the English coast and London from surprise French attack are further evidence of where the likely foe was suspected then to be.

Lord Salisbury was under some pressure, both in London and Berlin, to formalise the relationship with Germany. This he was loath to do, especially as German enmity was fiercer towards France than Russia and Britain was more likely to require German aid in the event of Russian animosity than of French belligerence. In any event, Lord Salisbury was not, by temperament, a believer in highly restrictive protocols, nor did he try to look too far ahead, preferring to react to his opponent's move rather than to initiate perilous large-scale strategies of his own. In a European world of unexpected quirks and fancies, it made pessimistic sense to him to treat cases on a purely individual basis. He might have appreciated the Noel Coward lyric, 'there is bad news just around the corner'.

He sometimes used the excuse of democratic governments being less able to guarantee promises that their replacements might not wish to honour. Ministers in the chancelleries of more despotic nations nodded sagely over this rejoinder,

Anglo-German Entente ... which was not to be

One of Germany's reasons for abandoning the Reinsurance Treaty [with Russia] had been the desire to avoid weakening what appeared to be a promising Anglo-German entente. In both countries there were influential people who regarded England and Germany as natural allies. This was the belief of Lord Salisbury and it was an article of faith for Joseph Chamberlain. On the German side, the desire to collaborate with the British was equally strong in many parts of society, but the German attitude towards Britain was always ambivalent. William II, for instance, who was a grandson of Queen Victoria, admired the British, but at the same time wanted to 'show them' that Germany was in no way inferior. The emperor's equivocal attitude was reflected in German foreign policy and had unfortunate results. ... By all odds, the most alarming German action was the decision to build a battle fleet. In 1896, in a speech delivered before the Colonial Society, William II announced that 'the future of Germany [was] on the sea'... There was, of course, no reason why Germany should not build a fleet. It was unreasonable, however, for the power with the greatest land army in Europe to begin serious competition with Britain on the seas and still to expect Britain to conclude some form of alliance. But men like Baron Holstein [the emperor's most influential foreign office counsellor] seem to have believed that Britain was a declining power (because of its performance in the Boer War), that it was confronted with a real possibility of war with Russia, that it needed allies more than it ever had, that its only possible alliance was with Germany, and that if Germany kept the pressure up, it would be willing to pay dearly for an agreement. This explains why British feelers for an alliance between 1899 and 1902 were always evaded adroitly by the Germans. The Germans were right in only one respect: the British were concerned about the drift of world events and were prepared to modify their past isolation by diplomatic agreements. But the British government had a wider choice of allies than was believed in Berlin. [Gordon A Craig, *Europe Since 1815* (Holt, Rinehart and Winston, New York: 1974) p 306f.]

conscious perhaps that the aristocratic Lord Salisbury admitted this weakness against his own better judgement of how such things should be organised. Bismarck, for one, was chary of the British capacity for keeping diplomatic promises, whilst his own swift removal from power in 1890 by the bellicose Kaiser Wilhelm II was a converse instance of the fragility of the political fabric. Nevertheless, Anglo-German friendship was believed to be a key element in the procurement and maintenance of a European concert. Opinion in both Berlin and London favoured the combine of a large German army and a large British navy as the most effective way of keeping the peace. Afterwards whispers of this notion were to be heard as late as just before the beginning and in the later stages of the Second World War.

Lord Salisbury was far from being an adventurer, well aware that Britain's interests continued to be best served by European peace. It is fair to add that the longheaded statesmen who headed the other large European powers were normally of the same view over this period. Lord Salisbury's political grasp of European affairs was guided by reference to the 1815 settlement at the end of the Revolutionary and Napoleonic Wars with France, when Lord Castlereagh, Britain's Foreign Secretary and Lord Salisbury's hero, had been to the fore in cementing a concord that, with a couple of exception, such as the Crimean War, had given widespread peace to Europe, and assuredly Britain for generations. Lord Salisbury had no illusions about this. *Our first duty*, he roundly said in a Guildhall speech, with a side-glance at the more ethically inclined Gladstone, *is towards the people of this country …our second is to all humanity*.[2]

He was eminently successful in this regard, believing

Our first duty is towards the people of this country …our second is to all humanity.

SALISBURY

that what he called *the community of Europe* was the key to Britain's safety. This, of course, was not a prophetic 'European Community' formula; it referred to the need for a concord of peace-loving nations across Europe, the occasional sparks of possible fires diplomatically hosed down by the ceaseless fire brigade activity at which he was so adept. Constantly finding a course between the inward-looking isolationist and the bloodthirsty Jingoist, he recognised that war was an element in the consideration. Contrary to some interpretations, he used the phrase *splendid isolation* ironically, recognising that conversations, even arguments, with one's neighbours were inevitable.

As the balance and the tempo of European politics altered, he was quick to promote the expenditure in 1889 of £21.5 million on ten more battleships and efforts were in train to make the navy a more homogenous striking force. Lord Salisbury never really trusted other nations: *where there is a liability to attack*; he asserted, *attack will come.*[3] It should again be emphasised that the perceived menace then was from the combined fleets of Russia and France. It is sometimes forgotten how sudden, in historical time, was the threat posed to Britain by Germany in its post-Bismarckian phase and how abrupt the switch by Britain to an Anglo-French (and thus indirectly Russian) entente in its post-Salisburyan era.

Certainly Lord Salisbury was successful in keeping Britain out of a continental war for another 20 or more years, extending the mainstream durability of the 1815 European settlement to approaching a hundred years, an avoidance of bloodshed for which generations of Britons could be thankful. Moreover, there was an honesty of aim in Lord Salisbury's ventures into foreign affairs. While he could be as duplicitous and secretive as any other diplomat in his tactics, his overall strategy of putting Britain first was, at least, free of the sanctimoniousness that occasionally besmirches some governmental pronouncements and actions about overseas relations. Lord Salisbury took the view that for *a sensitive commercial community*, such as Britain, security was paramount, whilst he was shrewd enough to recognise that the feeling of safety was as important as its reality.

As the 1882 Egyptian illustration described above indicates, Lord Salisbury's approach to the Empire was a gloss on his global view. Imperial domains, conquered or conquerable, were more pawns on the chessboard or balls on the snooker table of the diplomatic game. They were sometimes grounds for bitter argument and sometimes assets for shrewd exchange.

On another occasion, at the height of the 'Scramble for Africa', Salisbury said about his military advisors: *If these men had their way, they would soon be asking me to defend the moon against a possible attack from Mars.*

'Europeanisation' came, for the first time in human history, to produce a situation where practically all the land areas of the world were subject to forms of a single hegemony. The squabbles of the European powers that had first been located in and around their homelands, and then in regions such as the Middle and Near East, India and the Americas, were next transferred to the whole of Africa and the rest of Asia. It was not just a case of the British Empire causing problems; every self-respecting European state fancied itself as an empire-builder.

Lord Salisbury preferred what is sometimes termed 'informal' empire, that is, the commercial and strategic exploitation of areas without the bother of actually occupying and managing them. It fitted well with his partiality for unofficial agreements with continental powers, several of which bargains were of a colonial nature. His time at the India Office perhaps dissuaded him from further temptations into direct rule. He was not troubled by dreams, visions and theories of empire, even during that period when explorers and writers jostled elbow to elbow in selling noble ideas of the British imperial mission. As early as 1868 the *Spectator* had spoken earnestly of Britain's 'binding duty to perform highly irksome or offensive tasks' in carrying forward its God-given responsibility to bring civilised ways and Christianity to backward races. 'Who dies for England, sleeps with God', intoned the much mocked poet laureate and Salisbury enthusiast, Alfred Austin – an eerie sentiment for those who find themselves over a hundred years on faced by Islamic suicide bombers.

Lord Salisbury was free of such cant. Indeed, he rued the fact that it was often the impetuosity of excitable Gordonesque clones in sensitive situations that created the need for taking up arms. As in Europe, Lord Salisbury was not opposed to force, believing stoutly, for instance, that *India is held by the sword* – and there were 130,000 Anglo-Indian troops, inclusive of a third of the British regular army, plus 450,000 soldiers in the princely states, installed for that sole purpose. He referred somewhat disparagingly to the skirmishes necessary to keep the Empire intact as *merely the surf that marks the edge of the advancing waves of civilisation.* Sensibly, he always chose, where possible, the diplomatic route and the businessmen involved in colonial trading concurred in this peaceful attitude.

Alfred Austin (1835–1913) was an enthusiast of imperialism and admirer of both Disraeli and Salisbury; he published 20 volumes of poetry and was made Poet Laureate in 1896 'to general mockery'. The notorious lines about the illness of the Prince of Wales, later Edward VII, have often been attributed to him: 'Along the electric wire the message came:/ He is no better – he is much the same.'

The so-called 'Scramble for Africa' – an 1884 newspaper

coinage – was more of an amble for the unhurried Lord Salisbury. His moves were often defensive rather than offensive, made necessary, in his mind, by the predatory acts of other nations. Where possible he left it to the trading companies and their outposts to make the running, only interfering with diplomatic communiqués or martial show when other foreign powers seemed to be too pushy or indigenous peoples too unwelcoming. The flag followed the trade.

A neat illustration of Lord Salisbury's contribution was in 1890, when he agreed with Germany to swap, roughly speaking, Heligoland for Zanzibar. Anglo-German friction on the East African coast and hinterland had been acrimonious; the offer of the Baltic island of Heligoland, a British possession since 1814 but, since the cutting of the Kiel Canal in 1887, of increased interest to Germany, seemed kindly; sole authority over Zanzibar, and some related coastline, gave the British a valuable defensive site at the south-eastern gateway to Middle Eastern trade routes. Everyone was satisfied and in the doing of the deed the Anglo-German partnership was honoured. Queen Victoria, not a person usually associated with an enthusiasm for referenda, wished her 2,000 Heligolanders to be consulted, but Lord Salisbury demurred, suggesting that this democratic precedent might be cited for other regions, *even India*. The Empress of India, not amused by such startling prospects, was suitably chastened and grudgingly accepted the deal.

With smaller nations Lord Salisbury could afford to be more heavy-handed. Between 1888 and 1891, Portugal, apostrophised by Salisbury as *a most tiresome little power*,[4] was claiming and pressing rights in the Nyasaland and Zambesi areas. There were provocative incidents and Lord Salisbury, although prostrate with a debilitating attack of influenza during some of this critical time, did not hesitate to threaten war. The potential foe backed down and the resultant Anglo-Portuguese Zambesi Agreement of 1891 was very favourable to the British.

Lord Salisbury was ever the pragmatist. He would condemn slavery in the Sudan as readily as, where he felt the British interest imperilled, he would condone it in the American Confederacy. The disaster of Gordon at Khartoum was eventually avenged at the Battle of Omdurman in 1898 when 8,000 British troops and almost 18,000 Egyptian soldiers routed a Sudanese force almost 60,000 strong. This arose when these Anglo-Egyptian forces marched to release the pressure of severe native attacks on the Italian army in the region. As a demonstration of industrial efficiency, with railway trains and river steamers, as well as heavy artillery and Maxim guns rattling off hundreds of rounds in rapid succession, it was a chilling lesson. There were less than 500 British killed and wounded, while, according to some estimates, nearly 16,000 Sudanese were slain. Thus British authority over the Sudan and the Nile Valley was, as Kitchener had often wished, assured. Shortly afterwards the French attempted an abortive military errand, hopeful still of muscling into this important region. This military expedition reached Fashoda, on the

> **The Battle of Omdurman** (2 September 1898) was notable for the fact that a future British prime minister was present, and indeed participated in one of the battle's most famous episodes. Lieutenant Winston S Churchill of the 4th Hussars, attached to the 21st Lancers, took part in the regiment's charge towards the end of the battle, which unexpectedly took the lancers into a shallow depression packed with enemy warriors. After a brief but bloody melee, the lancers got clear, but out of 300 men, 70 had been killed and more wounded. Lieutenant Churchill was indeed lucky to have escaped unscathed.

Nile some 400 miles from Khartoum, but, fresh from his victory at Omdurman, Sir Herbert Kitchener promptly took offensive action. There was temporary stalemate and even the risk of war, but, once more, Lord Salisbury had read the runes aright; he had counted on the sympathy of the German and the frailty of the French governments and France yielded.

Lord Salisbury's seeming approval, on the other hand, of American slave-owning was linked to his fear of an unduly powerful north-led industrialised United States, his main worry, strange perhaps to modern ears, being that the USA might annex Canada. It is true that, as the century wore on, and what F J Turner called 'the vanishing frontier' of the USA disappeared into the Pacific Ocean, the Americans turned from the internal colonisation of their vast continent and gazed outwards. There were brushes with Lord Salisbury's administration over the USA's somewhat specious support of Venezuelan claims upon parts of British Guiana; there was watchfulness over the nascent Panama Canal enterprise (it was not opened until 1914) and, on practical grounds, there was strict neutrality when the USA went to war with Spain in 1898. Much as he detested the United States, Lord Salisbury, with many distractions in the Orient, was not to be drawn on relatively minor annoyances in the Occident.

The self-government of white settler colonies was a unique feature of British imperialism. Canada had become a Dominion in 1867, while New Zealand and the separate Australian colonies also enjoyed degrees of self-rule. New Zealand did not become a Dominion until 1907, while Australia was federated, under the ambit of Lord Salisbury's ministry, in 1901. Indeed, the first 56 Australian Test Cricket matches were actually played against teams drawn merely from three or four self-governing colonies, Victoria and New South Wales among them — although one touches on the complexities of cricketing geopolitics at some peril. Lord Salisbury, while not opposing Dominion status in such cases, did not believe it should be spread outside areas of English immigrant dominance. He was hopeful, too, that these thriving countries would contribute to their own defence, and, given the enormous sacrifices of Dominion troops in the Boer War and the two World Wars, he was not being overly optimistic.

It might be noted that, as the Far East and the Pacific Ocean became the focus for colonial wrangling and there were Australian forebodings about French and German advances in the Pacific. Lord Salisbury found himself thinking in terms of China and Japan. The value of Chinese imports from Britain by the end of the century was £33 million, compared with only £0.5 million for Russian imports. His caution over the Boxer Rising of 1900 against the Peking legations was fuelled by a dread that the other powers would react with expansionist designs in the Yangtze Basin, where Britain's commercial interests were uppermost, and the relief of the siege, without resort to full scale hostilities, appeared to justify his habitual wariness. As for Japan, in one of the last acts of his ministry he affirmed the negotiations of the Anglo-Japanese treaty of 1902, the first formal peacetime alliance agreed by Britain for generations. Its intention, principally through naval commitments, was to foil Russian intercession in the Far East.

Bechuanaland in 1885; Burma and Nigeria in 1886; Somaliland and Zululand in 1887; Kenya and Sarawak in 1888; barely a year passed at this stage without some eastern annexation. Dozens of quarrels and incidents occurred as the colonisation of Africa and, indeed, much of the Pacific was completed. The bargaining was intense. In 1890, for example, an agreement was reached with the French whereby there was mutual recognition of French authority in Madagascar and parts of northwest Africa and of British supremacy in the Zanzibar protectorate and other parts of East Africa. By the end of the century the British Empire covered a fifth of the world's land surface, a sum of 12 million square miles, three million square miles of which were chiefly the result of these recent African acquisitions. There were 400 million inhabitants, although no less than 300 million of these lived in India. There were about 10 million British settlers in the Canadian and Australasian regions, so that, with the home population, British stock accounted for less than one in ten of the entire imperial population.

Lord Salisbury's busy engagement with Empire was closely associated with the career of Joseph Chamberlain (1836–1914). This former radical mayor of Birmingham and former vituperative critic of the landed interest had been the ringleader of the anti-Home Rule revolt against William Gladstone. He was, by that token, a destroyer of the old Liberal Party, which good judges suggest he might otherwise have gone on to lead in a distinctly progressive fashion. As it was, he found himself the ally of his ancient enemy, Lord Salisbury. As leader of the Liberal Unionists in the commons, he exuded anticipation of great doings, especially as Lord Salisbury began his third administration, in 1895, entirely reliant on such support. He was offered the significant post of Chancellor of the Exchequer, but chose instead the Colonial Office, hitherto not regarded as a major department.

Joseph Chamberlain, enthusiastic, energetic and anxious to make a practical mark, soon altered that concept, throwing himself jubilantly into the business of opening up what he called the 'undeveloped estates'. Economic and social subventions in West Africa; steamship subsidies for the neglected West Indies – these were the kind of bustling reforms he introduced. He was much more of an imperial idealist than

Imperialism

In 1883, when Sir John Seeley published his enormously popular book *The Expansion of England*, he pointed to the growth of Russia and the United States and warned that within 50 years, they would have completely dwarfed states like France and Germany and would do that the same to Great Britain if its people continued to regard it as 'simply a European state'. A similar argument had already been made in France by Leroy-Beaulieu, who stated that colonial expansion was for his country 'a matter of life and death', and that, if France did not become a great African power, if was only a question of time before it was depressed to the position of Greece or Romania. The same thoughts were expressed in Germany, and in 1905, during the Moroccan crisis, some government figures actually desired war against France as the first step toward an effective imperial policy. These fears for the future were shared by most powers, and this increased the speed and the indiscriminateness of the process of acquisition. Moreover, the governments of Europe could not always control their own agents, who were often, in Lord Salisbury's words, *men of energy and strong will, but probably not distinguished by any great restraint over their feelings ... trying to establish by means which must constantly degenerate into violence the supremacy of that nation for which they were passionately contending.* These words well describe the breed of men who were the trailblazers of imperialism: men like the German explorer Carl Peters, who in the 1880s while still in his twenties, explored and acquired, by treaty with native chiefs, a domain of 60,000 square miles in East Africa; or like that strange blend of patriot, visionary, and businessman Cecil Rhodes (1853–1902). A clergyman's son, sent to Africa for his health, Rhodes made a fortune in the Kimberley diamond fields. For the rest of his life, he strove to 'advance the power of England' in Africa. Like Peters, Rhodes not infrequently believed that he knew better than the British government what his country's interests really were, and he was not disinclined to force its hand. His services to this country were great, but he must bear a large share of responsibility for the Boer War. [Gordon A Craig, *Europe Since 1815* (Holt, Rinehart and Winston, New York: 1974) p 289] his Prime Minister. Where Lord Salisbury found the ceremonial and junketing faintly wearisome, Joseph Chamberlain encouraged a colourful and vibrant imperial note to be struck at both the Queen's Jubilees of 1887 and 1897. There were many books and associations – for example, Sir John Seeley's *Expansion of England* (1883) and the Imperialist Federation League (1884) – available to back his strident opinion. He used the colonial conferences that were part of the two Jubilees to exhort the colonies to join in imperial union. This they abjured, having but recently edged towards self-government and, crucially, self-control of taxation. Chamberlain was also a foremost advocate of the doctrine of preferential 'fair trade' agreements with the Empire. His ambition was for a self-sufficient commonalty of regions, protected by tariffs, which would give Great Britain politico-economic security and prosperity.

While Lord Salisbury recognised the trading virtues of colonialism, he was not beguiled by such grandeur and waxed sardonically on the doubtful commercial allure of Africa. He was probably correct in his estimates. About 1900, a third of British exports went to the colonies, as opposed to over half to Europe and the Americas; only after 1900 did imports from the colonies begin to rise, but then only to about a quarter of the overall total by 1910. In any event, four-fifths of imperial imports came from India and the 'white' Dominions, and only a small proportion from the newer tropical acquisitions; similarly, three-fifths of British overseas investment went to foreign nations, whilst, of the remaining two-fifths that found its way to the colonies, almost all of it went to the 'old' Empire and not the new African and other settlements.

The price of Chamberlain's imperial gusto was his quietude about his more youthful attachment to domestic social reform. It was a price that the intractable Lord Salisbury was willing to pay. By and large, what superficially seemed an awkward partnership worked fairly smoothly, only to be harshly tested in the concluding years of the Salisbury third government, when the long-running ulcer of South Africa had to be lanced.

The British position in South Africa was, of course, confounded by the presence of determined Dutch settlers on what were regarded as British possessions. The situation was a complicated one. Following the Boers' defeat of a small British force at Majuba Hill in 1881, Transvaal had won back for itself a large measure of independence. Transvaal showed little affection for any unity under British sovereignty with the three other white-based units of the Orange Free State, also a chiefly Boer domain, Natal and the Cape Colony. This may have caused fewer problems had not Transvaal become the locale for a glittering gold rush, with the Uitlanders, as the Boers called the mainly British incomers, heavily taxed for their troubles by the Boer government and refused reasonable political rights.

This seething morass of mutual discontents was clearly demonstrated by the extremism of the two major adversaries. Cecil Rhodes was another of those over vaunting fanatics who so regularly earned Lord Salisbury's scorn. His dream had been not only of the British total annexation of the whole of Africa, but of British control of much of the middle east, tracts of the Pacific land areas, South America and eventual reunification with the United States. He was managing director of the South Africa Chartered Company (1889), yet another example of the semi-detached approach of using a trading concern, after the manner of the old East India Company (or, latterly, the similar agencies in Borneo, East Africa and Nigeria) as a joint political and commercial tool. Cecil Rhodes was also Prime Minister in Cape Town, so he also had a direct constitutional locus. He laid ambitious plans for a Cape to Cairo railway, although the German occupation of Tanganyika frustrated this scheme, and Cecil Rhodes was increasingly irritated by what he felt to be Boer transgressions. In the opposite corner was Paul Kruger, rugged and obdurate, the President of the Boer republic. Funded by the proceeds of the Witwatersrand gold-field, and with Johannesburg a boom city, he bought up armaments, recruited pro-German Dutch administrators and, in general, envisioned Boer supremacy in the south of the African continent.

Cecil John Rhodes (1853–1902) was one of the great empire-builders of the 19th century. Making a fortune in the South African diamond mines in the 1870s, by 1887 he controlled the De Beers mines. This success was turned towards territorial expansion into Bechuanaland and Matabeleland (later Rhodesia and now Zimbabwe) by his British South Africa Company. Prime Minister of the Cape in 1890, conflict with the Boers led to the disastrous Jameson Raid in 1895, and he was forced to resign. A lasting legacy of his are the Rhodes Scholarships.

These two dreams in collision produced a nightmare. First, in 1895 Rhodes' companion, L S Jameson, conducted his notorious armed 'raid' into the Transvaal, ostensibly to assist the Uitlanders in their plucky struggle. Apart from the overt illegality of the act, the signal failure of the Uitlanders to rebel on cue suggested that they did not think gold pickings without the franchise was unendurable. The accusations and counter-accusations, at home, in South Africa and throughout Europe, that followed this inglorious fiasco considerably darkened the atmosphere. Second, emboldened by the 'Kruger' telegram, in which the warlike and Anglophobe German Kaiser William II, congratulated the Boer leader on his bold and decisive handling of the Jameson raid, a truculent Boer stance was sustained in consequent discussions on the Uitlanders' condition. On its side, the British government was anxious not to be perceived as weak in its protection of its nationals overseas. It must also be added that the British High Commissioner in South Africa from 1897, Sir Arthur Milner, was not the most tactful of negotiators. The popular mood in both camps did nothing to dampen the inflammatory situation. Jingoism, patriotism's *bastard brother* in Lord Salisbury's contemptuous phrase, was noisy and obstreperous, especially in London.[5]

The South African war broke out in 1899, with the Boers taking the initiative. Their force of 60,000, including what many assessed as the world's best cavalry fighting on cavalry's best terrain, inflicted several defeats on the much smaller British army of 15,000. 'Black Week', just before Christmas of 1899, when the British suffered three separate reverses, marked the apogee of the Boer campaign. Thereafter the British mustered as many as 450,000 troops under the command of Lord Roberts and Kitchener. The Boers may have missed a trick by concentrating too much on static sieges and the defence of the Natal passes instead of sweeping down to and through Cape Colony and capturing Cape Town. Soon the mainstream fighting was finished; the Relief of Mafeking in May 1900 curiously gave vent to a 'crazy and unlovely carnival', particularly on the streets of London, which spoke more of nervousness banished than delight enjoyed.

Unluckily, there was the messy aftermath of Boer guerrilla tactics and the British riposte of destruction of Boer farms and the confinement of civilians, 20,000 of whom perished in concentration camps. It was 1902 before the Peace of Vereeniging brought a termination to these squalid episodes. The two Boer provinces were encompassed well and truly within the British Empire, albeit with offers of much needed practical aid and promises of future self-rule. In 1910 the four colonies combined as the Union of South Africa, thereby rendering open the status of the first 21 Anglo-South African cricket matches that took place before that date to some further searching geopolitical scrutiny.

The Boer War, despite ultimate victory, was an unsatisfactory conclusion to Lord Salisbury's authoritative command of British overseas affairs: 8,000 British and imperial soldiers were killed, 13,000 died of disease and 21,000 were wounded, and the war cost an expensive £270 million. This was not one of the 'little wars' to which the British public had become habituated. It had not been another Omdurman. The public mood was sombre. The one compensating aspect was that Lord Salisbury's shrewd avoidance of continental entanglement had held good. In particular, the Germans, for all Kruger's hopes and overtures, resolutely refused to be drawn into the conflict. The British fleet off the coast of East Africa reminded the Germans of where the dominant maritime strength still lay. For all that, the tide was turning, as the Kaiser and his advisers had embarked on a phase of naval construction after 1898 that was predicated on rivalling the British fleet. The Salisbury ministries had been quick to repair the alleged slackness of the Gladstone administrations in this regard. In 1889 the 'Two-Power Standard' had been adopted, its aim for the Royal Navy to keep afloat more than the joint number of ships of the next two largest fleets. At that juncture the two navies in question had been the Russian and French fleets; a dozen years later, it was the German and American navies, although it was not anticipated, as in the former instance, that there was any chance of an alliance of those two nations.

Whatever the case, Lord Salisbury's policy of the veiled threat of war or, at last resort, the fighting of a limited campaign, had been found wanting in South Africa, with the army found seriously defective against a well-armed and bellicose force of European extraction. There was a feeling that there had been an over-emphasis on rebuilding the navy at the expense of an army that seemed to be, by Continental standards, weak at many levels. Moreover, Lord Salisbury's long emphasis on friendship with Germany, a policy of which Joseph Chamberlain was a wholehearted supporter, was showing signs of wear and tear. There were contingent reports of some change in British attitudes, with the centuries old antipathy for France, if not evaporating, being at least partially replaced by ill-feeling toward Germany, with a hearty reciprocation from the German side. Lord Salisbury, as he retired, unfit and ageing, from office, must have felt even gloomier than usual about the brutishness of men, especially those of an alien breed.

Like Russian dolls, Lord Salisbury's policies on Ireland, the Empire and the world at large fitted snugly into one another. Ireland was part of the Empire, just as the importance of the Empire was its part in the global machinations of the great powers. The thought of an independent neighbouring polity, especially perhaps one – the Irish bishops were, according to Salisbury, *Home Rulers in action* – of Roman Catholic persuasion, was a fearful one. Ireland would become, in Salisbury's trenchant phrase, *a rickety and crazy republic* – and he cited the precedent of the independent Boers purchasing arms from friendly powers. The Protestant settlers in Ulster, no less the Anglican landowners in the south of Ireland, were akin to English pioneers in Africa or the Middle East; they were entitled to British protection.

There was the question of apparent weakness. Lord Salisbury was very conscious that an aspect of his task was to create an illusion of British potency. He believed that any yielding to a violent and recalcitrant Irish peasantry would have been judged across Europe as a signal that Great Britain was creaking and feeble and that incursions into British controlled possessions might be attempted. Ceding ground to the Irish was as risky as permitting the Uitlanders to be bullied by the surly Boers.

To the proposal that Ireland might be treated like Canada and granted a major element of self-governance, he preferred to draw the analogy of India, where he believed *the elective principle* was inappropriate. Lord Salisbury was as racialist as most other Victorian English gentlemen and even by the standards of the day he was very plain-spoken. In his descending ethnic ladder, the 'Teutonic' races were on the top rung, a credo that underpinned his taste for friendship with Germany. The Irish were barely above the lowest step. Free institutions did not suit everyone, thought Lord Salisbury, and he mentioned Hottentots, Indians, Russians and Irishmen as examples. The Irish, he explained, were *habituated to the use of knives and slugs* and thus unfitted for freedom. Their country was, in any event, split into *two deeply divided and antagonistic nations* and not susceptible to constitutional reform. The English gentry on both sides of the Irish Sea shared Lord Salisbury's view that Gladstone's Home Rule venture set the masses against the classes, with its intimation that the Irish lower orders might expect some degree of political leverage. As Lord Salisbury had been opposed to the extension of the British franchise to the unpropertied social groups, it was not likely he would accept measures of civil rights in Ireland. The large majority of the Irish failed the acid political test on ethnic, religious and economic grounds.

Having read a little law as a young man, Lord Salisbury constantly turned to a narrow interpretation of the law of contract to support his views and he had long been horrified by the infringement of that legal concept in successive attempts to ameliorate the harsh lot of the Irish tenants. Moreover, his preservation of the Conservative supremacy on the mainland, after the buffeting of largely Liberal ministries since the Peelite betrayal of the 1840s, was wholly dependent on the support of the Liberal Unionists. Led by Joseph Chamberlain in the commons and the Marquess of Hartington, later the Duke of Devonshire, in the Lords, the Unionists had siphoned off Liberals from both the radical and Whig wings of the party. Lord Salisbury was cleverly content to play the cards that pictured anarchy, civil war and economic decline in Ireland should Home Rule be granted. As always, his preferred option was the avoidance of needless reaction.

The presence of a large troupe of Irish Nationalist MPs in parliament was a nuisance, to the point that some Tories wavered on the edge of a shift to Home Rule purely for the reason that they would be rid of this encumbrance. The Conservatives blundered badly in 1887, when they became involved in a *Times* exposure of Parnell's connection with the Phoenix Park murders of Lord Frederick Cavendish and W H Burke; the critical letters turned out to be the forgeries of one Richard Pigott. However, the Tory government was crucially helped by the domestic scandal that broke over Parnell's head in 1889 when his long-term adulterous relationship with Kitty O'Shea became open knowledge to a moralising, gossiping British populace. He died in 1891 and the chains that bound the Irish Nationalists to the sober-sided Nonconformist Liberals were broken.

This much eased the parliamentary aspect of Lord Salisbury's job. Lord Salisbury's nephew and successor as premier, Arthur Balfour, won his spurs as Ireland's Chief Secretary, dealing out a mix of coercion and concession with imperturbable flair, despite being branded 'Bloody' Balfour by his angry opponents. He skilfully carried through both stern criminal

(1887) and helpful land purchase (1891) legislation. Later his brother, Gerald Balfour, was appointed Chief Secretary and he introduced a further land act in 1896 and an act of 1898 that introduced county councils to Ireland. The former measure supplied £36 million for tenants' purchase of their farms and smallholdings, while the latter act, predictably, led to the election of over 500 Nationalist county councillors against 125 Unionists, the majority of these in Ulster.

Arthur James Balfour (1848–1930), was Lord Salisbury's nephew and his successor as Prime Minister. A brilliant intellectual, with interests in science and philosophy, he entered Parliament in 1874 and was his uncle's private secretary. In 1887 he was Chief Secretary for Ireland. When Salisbury resigned in 1902, Balfour became Prime Minister, but was decisively defeated in the General Election in 1905. He continued in politics, however, serving in the First World War coalition government as Foreign Secretary and held further offices up until the 1920s. (See *Balfour* by Ewen Green, in this series.)

As the years dragged on the atmosphere over Ireland, while still sullen, was calmer. Especially with the retirement and death (1898) of Gladstone, the chance of a successful Home Rule bill was remote. As for Lord Salisbury, he was not at all keen on either the land or the governmental reforms, believing that they raised false hopes of Home Rule in Irish breasts. He felt obliged, with the utmost reluctance, to allow such legislation to go forward as sops, not so much to the Irish people, as to the Liberal Unionists on whose support he relied.

Frequently misanthropic about his fellow men, Lord Salisbury had a poor opinion of the Irish landlords, whom he regarded as *troublesome and unreliable allies*. The fact that the largest landowners were Whigs may have contributed to this assessment. For instance, the Whig Marquess of Lansdowne had 130,000 acres in Ireland, whereas many of the smaller landlords, with, say, 10,000 to 30,000 acres, were Tories, including, among others, ex-army officers. Lord Salisbury, an inveterate sufferer from seasickness, never visited Ireland until 1890 and thereafter rarely. His views, then, were usually prompted purely by English concerns; he had, for instance, a willing ear to the worries of English Conservative land-owners who wondered whether Irish land legislation might be copied in England. What with the agrarian depression and the stirrings of trade unionism among the agricultural labour-force, they were anxious about Irish agitation and similar responses being transferred to English farmlands.

Lord Salisbury was neither the first nor the last British politician to believe that the Irish problem was unremit-ting. He was quietly pleased that he had, at least for a while, smothered the flames. Both landlords and tenants were tem-porarily subdued.

By such means and on such considerations did Lord Salisbury survey the outside world, with a magisterial suavity, for the better part of two decades. This left him little time for that for which he had, in truth, little inclination: the business of home affairs.

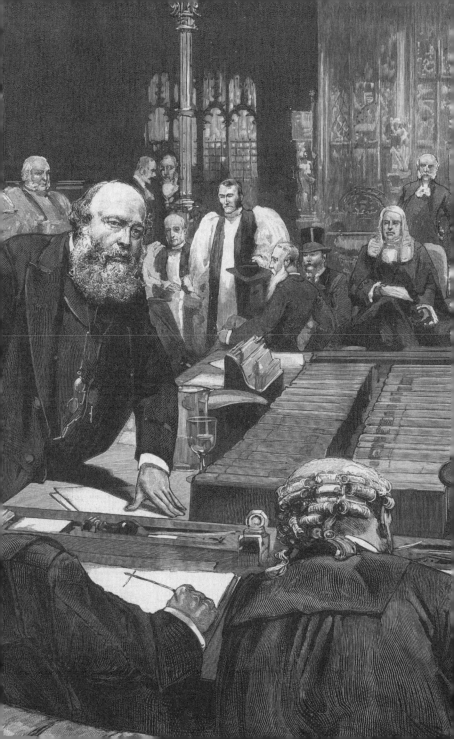

Chapter 5: Lord Salisbury at Home

The clever world is very intolerant of plain, practical statesmen. It maintains, sometimes with very good reason, that where the imagination is stunted, it is merely because the whole mind is stunted, too; and that the claim to practical common sense is often only a euphemism for a narrow intelligence straitened by an abject regard for precedent and routine. [1]

The spirited efforts by his modern biographers to resurrect the reputation of Lord Salisbury have discovered that their most difficult chore lies in reinterpreting his domestic record. It is hard to drum up a case for Lord Salisbury as a social reformer. The suggestion by one historian that the Workmen's Compensation Act passed under his jurisdiction heralded the beginnings of the Welfare State is a sign of the panic engendered by such a thought process.

The genuine Welfare State, envisioned as the converse of the 'Warfare' State of the Fascist and Stalinist dictatorships of the 1930s, was founded in 'universalism', the notion that all should give that all might benefit. Lord Salisbury would have had no truck with William Beveridge's ideal that such a society was 'desirable to foster social solidarity and feelings of identity'. A firmer case could be made for the Elizabethan Poor Law Settlement of 1601 as being a progenitor of the Welfare State than any enactment for which Lord Salisbury was responsible.

Lord Salisbury had a strong faith in a weak state. When the state was well equipped with a purposeful bureaucratic apparatus funded by heavy taxation, then were the landed and allied interests at some hazard should opponents grab hold of these dynamic instruments. Lord Salisbury voiced the paradox, *the feebleness of our government is our security*. One could not be shot by an unloaded pistol.

Lord Salisbury was Prime Minister at a time when there were pronounced social stirrings, apart from the violence in Ireland. Organised leftwing and working class agencies were developing. The Social Democratic Federation (1884), partly Marx-inspired; the influential and intellectual Fabian Society (1884); the Independent Labour Party (1893) and, finally, the Labour Representation Committee (1900), the source of the Labour Party, were all evidence of this tendency. The craft trade unions had satisfactorily survived the economic tempests of the age, while the development of 'general' or unskilled workers' unionism moved on apace. There were two million trade unionists by the end of the 19th century. The minor disturbances of February 1886, following a procession of the unemployed workers in London; 'Bloody Sunday', in November 1887, when socialists and police clashed bitterly in London; the dramatic match girls' strike at Bryant and May in 1888, and the successful London dockers' strike of 1889 – such impelling and emblematic events struck chords with both political left and right

Lord Salisbury took such warnings of portending class war seriously, perhaps too seriously. At every twist and turn of the political process he prophesied that the class war had been declared – the Liberal victory of 1880 caused him to

The feebleness of our government is our security.

SALISBURY

talk earnestly about a *serious war of the classes*. His response was to try and win it. Not for Lord Salisbury was there any pussyfooting around with 'one nation' Toryism. He viewed with some scorn the previous endeavours of Sir Robert Peel and Benjamin Disraeli to associate the Conservatives with progressive social reforms. In the event, Disraeli's efforts in this direction had not been as magnificent as the advance publicity; after some useful reforms in the first two sessions of his 1874/80 ministry, relating chiefly to schooling and public health, the well had quickly run dry. They compared unfavourably with the dynamic work of the preceding Liberal administration that had wrought substantial structural changes in fields such as education, the army, the civil service and judicial matters.

Lord Salisbury rejected collectivist thinking out of hand. His view was that the divide between the classes should be reinforced, so that the rich fraction prospered and the masses should be persuaded, by fear if necessary, that revolutionary politics would be counter to even their scanty material interests. It will be recalled that this alarmist approach was one of the lines he took with reference to Ireland. Lord Salisbury clearly understood that social revolution only truly succeeded when the elite, in his word, *collapsed*; he was determined that this would not happen in Britain.

There have been some whispers among commentators that Lord Salisbury's anti-state position presaged the strategy of Margaret Thatcher's administrations. This grants inadequate credit to Lord Salisbury's profounder grasp of societal mechanics than that of his resolute successor. Although the Thatcher ministries declared open range for rampant money-making and unashamed individualism, many social historians would agree that these were heavily centralising governments. They found themselves in what might, at its extremes, be called 'the Pinochet paradox'. Inexorably wedded to privatism, they found it necessary to construct strict central disciplines to preserve that often tense situation. The police were well nigh nationalised, local government was neutered by the withdrawal of funding and regulation to the centre, while the suffocating blanket of a national curriculum and sundry tight regulations strangulated even the nation's children. Lord Salisbury was more subtle and multifaceted in his defence of his political values. He opted for a shrewdly-managed cluster of checks and balances; he would never have risked bequeathing so heavy-handed an instrumentality to a potentially more progressive replacement.

Thus his negative attitude to domestic reform, whilst minimalist, was not absolute. A paternalist, and one who looked to the leaders of industry and business to be as paternalist as the wiser landlords, he recognised the need for the occasional excursion into governmental remedies. While never wholly blind to the sheer horror of those aspects of Victorian existence that gave rise to what was termed the 'intolerabilty' theory and the sheer necessity for some amelioration, his leading intention was inoculation. His hope was that, in the last resort, small doses of amendment would cure the diseases.

The 1897 Workmen's Compensation Act falls into this category. He acknowledged that the *claims of mere liberty* should not be allowed to *endanger the lives of citizens* and he was prepared to stand up to the irate opposition of the coal owners and others.[2] This was an instance where sordid profiteering denied many workers reasonable safeguards. Joseph Chamberlain, the chief advocate of this measure, dismissed, with the brusque realism of the Birmingham businessman, any hocus-pocus about the legalistic niceties of negligence. He insisted that accidents were a cost on the industry and should, therefore, be paid by the industry. Although some kinds of accidents and some major occupational categories – merchant seamen, domestic servants, agricultural labourers – were excluded, onus of proof for accidents at work passed from the employee to the employer, who henceforward was obliged to adopt some kind of an insurance scheme. During the coming years even the exceptions were brought into line with the general law.

The passage of the measure also has to be seen in the context of Lord Salisbury keeping Joseph Chamberlain on side. Given the vibrant radical promise that Chamberlain brought to the 'virtual coalition', it was, surprisingly, the ministry's sole social reform of any telling impact. It was a sorry outcome after all Chamberlain's vigorous campaigning on a raft of basic social issues. Joseph Chamberlain's enthusiasm for old age pensions, for example, was soon lost and abandoned in a labyrinth of enquiries and reports, while his attention was constantly diverted towards colonial questions. It is also note-worthy that accident compensation, unlike old age pensions, did not directly burden the state financially. Lord Salisbury, tepid, by that token, on the subject of pensions, preferred some flexibility in the locally financed poor rate for 'aged paupers'. Many Conservatives regarded pensions as 'the most dangerous of all forms of state socialism', so Lord Salisbury was by no means alone in his caution about what he curtly described as *the predatory principle of legislative benevolence*. Furthermore, the excessive cost of the South African War ended any thoughts of 'legislative benevolence'. Income tax, which had been held at 8d (3p) jumped to a calamitous 1s (5p) in the pound.

The Salisbury governments' attitude to the land and farming is another good illustration of the Prime Minister's distaste for domestic reform. Prior to the 1885 general election Joseph Chamberlain had crusaded on the basis of his 'unauthorised programme', the ringing tones of which had horrified Queen Victoria and many others. Among its tenets was a radical scheme of land reform, a topic that has never been more strongly aired politically than in these months. 'What ransom will property pay for the security which it enjoys?' asked Chamberlain as the landed interest jibbered in dread. He argued that local authorities should be enabled to buy up land compulsorily at fair prices, in the towns to improve housing and planning standards, and in the countryside for a supply of smallholdings to the rural proletariat. His Birmingham associate, Jesse Collinge, coined the slogan 'three acres and a cow'. Such was the resonance of this appeal that, even 50 years on in the 1930s, the effervescent comedian, Max Miller, could utilise it for one of his typically jaunty anti-feminist gags, the total comprehension of a variety theatre audience guaranteed. (Purely in the interests of completing the record, the joke ran: 'when I got married her father promised me three acres and a cow ... I'm still waiting for the three acres ... 'ere'.)

Max Miller obtained more mileage out of the maxim than the Victorian farm labourers. The results of the 1887 Allotments Act and the Smallholdings Act of 1892 were minute in scale. They allowed for county councils to establish such letting schemes, but they were permissive and suffered from lack of capital, advice and the other features essential to agricultural success. Although allotments gradually became a marginal feature of English life, there was no fundamental land reform. In 1905 the constitutional lawyer, A V Dicey, remarked on what he called 'the paradox of the land law'; that is, the way in which, in spite of notional democratisation, property regulation was still 'appropriate to an aristocratic state'.

One overwhelming consequence of Gladstone's Home Rule agitation, with the likes of Jesse Collinge joining Chamberlain in the Liberal Unionist lobby, was the disruption of the campaign to modernise land ownership. This was largely true of urban as of rural land. The Housing of the Working Classes Act of 1890, with clauses for the assimilation and clearance of slum areas, was also permissive and subject to the resistance of landlords. It codified the procedures by which urban authorities might borrow money for housing replacement, although many towns and cities were prohibited by the high on-costs and there were no national housing subsidies available. It was difficult in this climate to balance the expensiveness of land against the sort of cheap rents that rehoused slum-dwellers might afford. Although there were the beginnings of efficient building standards, overcrowding remained at high levels and there was, as yet, no general acceptance of municipal housing as a social measure. As late as 1914, only 0.5 per cent of the housing stock was of local authority build, the majority of it – about 50,000 units – in London. There was an act passed in 1899 that made loans available to solvent artisans for the purchase of private properties but it was not much employed.

Amid the agrarian depression of those years, the Agricultural Land Rating Act of 1896 halved the rates payable by owners and occupiers of agricultural land, with the deficit made up by subsidies of £3.5 million from taxation. This, of course, brought little benefit to the farm labourers, except in that their employers' prospects were boosted. In a revealing moment, Walter Long, just the second incumbent of the recently created if mainly dormant agriculture department, suggested that this subsidisation of landowners and farmers was the nearest possible return to the 'protection' of the antiquated Corn Laws. The counterpoise of subsidies for farmers but not for urban slum dwellers is a mark of Lord Salisbury's priorities and his anxiety to preserve the landed interest. Predictably, he was an opponent of indirect taxes that bore heavily on landowners. Death duties legislation he thought of as *a law of grievous hardship and oppression*. Apropos social reform, Lord Salisbury was a winner on two fronts. His absorption of the Liberal Unionists into Tory ranks meant that he was able, for a generation, to postpone two of his most feared outcomes; Irish independence and excess social reform at home. The relatively tiny changes he agreed assuaged what had been a gargantuan appetite for improvement among sufficient Chamberlainite Unionists to keep them loyal to the Salisbury coalition.

Lord Salisbury never strayed from his pronounced church-state principles. His devotion to regular holy communion and his solemn theological creed apart, he was enamoured of the functional quality of the established church, which he saw as an ever-present bulwark against the abrasiveness of class conflict. Anglicanism for Salisbury was, wrote Michael Bentley, 'not only a religion but a civic pact with previous generations'. Thus Lord Salisbury took very seriously questions to do with the appointment of bishops, with church discipline and with similar matters of what might seem to the secular mind to be of arcane concern. Typically, he could be as critical of the personnel of an institution as he would toil endlessly for its sustenance. Just as he upbraided his fellow landlords, his party colleagues, his fellow lords and even, on occasion, the monarch, he was rather dismissive of E W Benson, Archbishop of Canterbury during most of Lord Salisbury's terms in office. Nonetheless, he struggled manfully to maintain the church's place in the political sun.

His detestation of Dissent bordered, in consequence, on hatred. It was the halfway house to outright heathenism, *the earthworks and blockhouse*, in Lord Salisbury's own scathing words, *for the maintenance of an untiring political guerrilla*, his accent again on the earthly rather than the supernatural designs of Nonconformity. These were years when the disestablishment of the English church was vigorously mooted. The Anglican Church in Ireland, what Gladstone had called 'the token and the symbol of the ascendancy', was disendowed in 1869 and Liberal demands for the disestablishment of the Welsh church were mounting. When Anthony Trollope used a measure to disestablish the Church of England as a central theme in his political novel *Phineas Redux*, published in 1874, he was not being at all facetious. Lord Salisbury had some cause to be apprehensive.

An instance of Lord Salisbury's dogged adherence to the Anglican cause is his pursuit of tithes reform. Against a joint tide of protest and indifference, he pushed through the 1891 Tithe Rent-charge Act, intended to ease the collection of the 10 per cent tax on land for the beneficed clergy, and a similar measure in 1899 that relieved vicars of rates due on tithe income, with the state reimbursing half the cost to the local authorities. This, like the Agricultural Rating Act, was an attempt to bolster by state means what Lord Salisbury thought to be significant elements in the struggle for constitutional control. These were unpopular pieces of legislation; tithes were an annoyance to many, especially, for example, Welsh Nonconformists, whose belligerent refusal to pay required the presence of troops in Wales in 1887/8.

However, it was the educational question that had the most far-reaching effects in so far as Lord Salisbury's involvement with the church was concerned. In 1885, he fulminated against *the lifeless, boiled-down, mechanical, unreal religious teaching* of the local board schools. The Liberals were keen to accelerate a decline in the church schools. Nonconformists, indeed many noncommittal English parents, were, on the whole, happy with, by dint of the compromise of the 1870 Education Act, the deliberately non-sectarian religious diet of the board schools, where a hymn, a prayer and some bible reading was closer to the heart of Dissent than to the more ritualistic needs of the Anglican and Roman Catholic schools. Impatient to sustain the Anglican schools as part of his construct of the Christian state in action, Lord Salisbury looked for ways to aid them. Lord Sandon's Education Act of 1876, albeit a Conservative measure, had been passed with the support of W E Forster, Liberal author of the seminal 1870 legislation that had created the school boards. The 1876 measure made elementary schooling compulsory. With the help of A J Mundella's 1880 Liberal measure, there were, by the time of Lord Salisbury's premiership, attendance by-laws in place in all local authority areas.

Society was then faced with a conundrum that Lord Salisbury found not to his taste. As he pointed out, the parents of three school-age children might be obliged to find 30s (£1.50) annually out of a possible income of only £60, and yet he regarded with anathema any attempt to relieve parents of the God-given duty to support their offspring responsibly. In 1891 Lord Salisbury grudgingly accepted the logic of the case that, if the state made schooling compulsory, it must then make it free. However, he was chiefly moved by the knowledge that, were his Liberal opponents to have the chance so to do, it was likely that they would make education free of charge only in publicly-funded board schools, leaving the church schools in perhaps terminal disarray. The Liberals, Lord Salisbury told his followers, *would deal with it in such a manner that the voluntary schools would be swept away*. He did not readily accept the principle involved, but, again, he had both avoided more drastic law-making and retained the backing of the Unionist radicals, chief among them the Unitarian Joseph Chamberlain.

In 1896 Lord Salisbury supported plans to remit more funds to church schools in return for some degree of local authority management, but this measure collapsed in the face of opposition from practically all sides. In 1897 some small steps were taken in helping with the salaries of church school staffs. Apart from the disapproval of dissenting and secular voices, there was always the side issue, one not lost on Lord Salisbury, that any amelioration of Anglican schools implicitly assisted Roman Catholic schools. Some Anglican church leaders felt Lord Salisbury was misguided in concentrating on the schools, believing, with some shrewdness, that the Church of England should turn its major attention to teacher training.

The major 1902 Education Act was passed early in A J Balfour's ministry, but the discussions began under Lord Salisbury's supervision. He worried that it might not be sufficiently protective of the church schools, but his anxiety was unduly aroused. The 1899 Cockerton Judgement had found that some proactive school boards, much frowned upon by the Tories, had overstepped the legal mark and were providing other than elementary education – at a time when the chance of elementary schoolchildren receiving grammar school education was four in a thousand. This was the spur for the vengeful destruction of the boards. The 1902 Act disbanded the 2,568 school boards and 700 school attendance committees, admittedly a collection of all shapes, sizes and conditions, and substituted 328 local education authorities based on local governmental boundaries. The act made what came to be known as primary and secondary schooling the responsibility of these local authorities. It was a further shift away from the Victorian penchant for single-purpose to the modern affection for multi-purpose authorities; the former, while they produced some erratic results, did often have the advantage of enthusiastic focus.

The other two elements of the bill were to switch the sensible school board emphasis on technical and vocational learning to an elitist, what nowadays would be termed a meritocratic, stress on grammar schools and thereby a selection process. Their rejuvenation was such that the number of grammar schools rose from barely a hundred in the late 19th century to 1,616 in 1925 and their average number of pupils had doubled to 300. At this stage only a quarter of the 340,000 pupils at what H G Wells called these 'caste-factories' enjoyed free places.

Robert Morant, 'the assassin of the boards', was the administrative genius behind this movement, which had the support of Oxford-trained neo-Platonists and also high-minded Fabians. Both were attracted by the structural rationalism of the reform and also perhaps by the dangerous 'selection' implications of eugenics in both its ethnic and social forms. Adrian Woolridge, in his 1997 study of the history of psychology and education, has asserted that the crude 'social Darwinism' of eugenics was in the opening decades of the 20th century 'the political correctness of its day'. The belief that one could and should test and separate children intellectually was the natural and unpleasant consequence.

Politically, the transfer of educational oversight favoured the Conservative Party – and there was a further twist to the plot. To the horror of the Nonconformists, especially in Wales – 'Rome has been put on the rates', cried David Lloyd George – the dual system of state and church schools was maintained, now under the novel nomenclature of 'provided' and 'non-provided' schools. Although Balfour was to complain that he had not realised 'the act would mean more expense and more bureaucracy' and although his Uncle Robert was still not entirely satisfied with the treatment of the church schools, the outcome was socially disastrous. The act amounted, despite its apparent rationality, to a major setback for any progress toward common schooling for all children, one devoid of either social or religious division. A J Mundella the Younger concluded, with some truth, that the 1902 Act was designed to 'eliminate, as far as possible, the democratic element'.[3] This had a political as well as a social connotation. It spelt the beginnings of a drift to a more concentrated central control that would be well consolidated a century later.

George Bernard Shaw's character, Cusins, in his play *Major Barbara*, first staged in 1905, echoed some of the thinking of Salisbury, Balfour and especially the politically adroit Morant; 'I want a democratic power strong enough to force the intellectual oligarchy to use its genius for the common good.'

The arrangements proposed by the 1902 Education Act, with which Lord Salisbury had but a transient interest, would have been unpractical without the local government reforms earlier associated with his administrations. Here again his hopes were favoured by a conjunction of what appeared to be rational and what was, in real terms, also politically advantageous. Lord Salisbury, as his negotiations with Gladstone's ministry over the redistribution of parliamentary seats had amply demonstrated, had an arithmetical flair and a sharp political acumen when faced with such tasks.

The 1835 Municipal Incorporation Act had brought some semblance of efficient supervision to the major towns and, in the wake of the parliamentary reform legislation, there was a desire to modernise the governance of the rural areas. At this point, the counties were ruled by the magistrates meeting at the quarter sessions, with an underpinning of the hundreds of parish vestries. The 1888 Local Government and County Electors Acts created a system of county councils with a franchise like that used in the boroughs, that is, eligibility by residence, occupation or rate-paying, each of a year's duration.

The county boundaries remained, by and large, the old-time shire frontiers, with the major exception that a complementary series of 61 'county boroughs' were established with similar powers to those of the county councils. This had a series of effects. There was a separation, in somewhat oversimplified terms, of urban radicals and rural reactionaries, rather to their mutual delight. However, as the counties grew in power, adding, for instance, education to their portfolio, the smaller non-county boroughs tended to be a trifle swamped often by Tory shires. Moreover, the segregation of the larger towns and cities away from their hinterland had the effect of robbing regions politically of their natural and frequently enterprising 'capital' cities.

Lord Salisbury typically found a golden mean between those such as Joseph Chamberlain and Lord Randolph Churchill, then very popular among the Conservative rank and file, who were keen on fundamental reform, and the squires and magistrates of the shires who were alarmed by these avant-garde, spendthrift prospects. Thus, as well as retaining the old borders and isolating the radical conurbations, he refused proposals for district councils on which 'parish radicals' might have muddied the deep blue waters of rustic calm. It was left to a Liberal enactment of 1894 to construct a network of parish, urban district and rural district councils to complete the overhaul of the ancient local governmental system of England and Wales.

What is more, when the county councils were formed,

Lord Salisbury insisted on the county police forces being left in the hands of the JPs, as they had been since their inauguration under the Police Acts of 1839 and 1856. Lord Salisbury explained to Chamberlain that *the civilisation of many English counties is sufficiently backward to make it hazardous for the crown to part with power over the police.*[4] The poor law administration, last and strongest of the single purpose authorities, survived until the inter-war years, when the counties and boroughs absorbed most of its functions.

The outcome was comforting to the Prime Minister. The forces of inertia, often evident in studies of administrative history, were compelling. It is true that, on the one hand, Wales was largely lost to the Tories, while London boasted a new London County Council with normally an impressive progressive majority. Lord Salisbury's ministers did something to trim these reddish sails with the 1899 London Government Act. This created 28 Metropolitan Borough Councils, several of them with natural Tory majorities, thereby considerably reducing the ambit of LCC powers.

On the other hand, the county scene was very little changed. There were actual contests in only a minority of counties at the first elections; the landlords-cum-magistrates who had ruled through the quarter sessions county courts

Lord Randolph Churchill (1849–95) was the third son of the 7th Duke of Marlborough and entered Parliament in 1874, the year he married the American heiress Jennie Jerome. Their son Winston (see *Churchill* by Chris Wrigley, in this series) was born later the same year. One of the leading Conservative politicians of his day, in 1886 he was made Chancellor of the Exchequer, but resigned in a dispute over military expenditure. Far from forcing Lord Salisbury to give in to him, this brought his political career to an end. He died in 1895 after a long illness.

comprised the bulk of the new councillors and aldermen; in 28 counties the previous chairman of the magistrates or the Lord Lieutenant was chosen as first chairman of the county council. Lord Salisbury had demonstrated again how opportunistic he could be in indulging his radical compatriots by undertaking a much sought after Liberal measure and giving it a reactionary tweak.

Allotments, schools, councils – such were the offerings of Lord Salisbury's sparse home programme during his three administrations. A J P Taylor wrote that, domestically, Salisbury espoused 'the outlook of a slow-witted countryman'. Lord Salisbury might

The use of Conservatism is to delay changes till they become harmless.

SALISBURY

have risked a smile at that insult, although he preferred to think of himself as *a policeman*, maybe a stolid village bobby, faced with what he called *workers of mischief*. His domestic programme reflected the dictum he privately defined in 1892: *the use of Conservatism is to delay changes till they become harmless.*[5] His supreme ability in the forging of Conservatism as an anti-progressive instrument is the subject of the next chapter.

Chapter 6: Lord Salisbury and Conservatism

By a free country, I mean a country where people are allowed, so long as they do not hurt their neighbours, to do as they like. I do not mean a country where six men may make five men do exactly as they like.[1]

As titular leader of the Conservative Party for the better part of 20 years, Lord Salisbury thought hard about and worked hard upon the nature of the beast on which he was saddled. He famously said that *if the Conservatives abandoned the principles for which I joined them, I should walk for the last time down the steps of the Carlton Club without casting a glance of regret behind me.*[2] He avoided this fate by constantly adapting the Conservatives to the principles to which *he* believed *they* should be heir. The Conservative Party was a tool for anti-progress; on the whole, he acted, in these years, as sole assessor of what was practical to this end, compromising, in niggardly, gingerly fashion, when necessity demanded. Sometimes this meant, as we have observed, the denial of a lesser precept for what he deemed the greater good. When, for example, the reform of the counties was inevitable, he insisted on the change being as pro-Conservative, in his terms, as possible. In practice, it engaged him in the dexterous handling of the several organs that comprised the body politic.

When Lord Salisbury embarked on his second ministry, he

was faced with two personnel problems. One, in respect of Joseph Chamberlain, has already been examined; the result was an affable working relationship between the two politicians. The other was Lord Randolph Churchill, the darling of the Tory backbenches and local activists. He had come to dominate the House of Commons, casting into the shade the much less ebullient Sir Stafford Northcote and thereby assisting, with some irony, the ascent of Lord Salisbury.

Randolph Churchill, the adored if aloof father of Winston, gathered about him a small group, including Arthur Balfour, that identified itself somewhat pretentiously as 'the Fourth Party'. They promulgated the notion of 'Tory democracy', a concept that Lord Salisbury would not have been alone in regarding as oxymoronic. Randolph Churchill was cynically vague on its definition, but it contrived to appeal to a Disraeli-like spread of lively action at home and spirited deeds abroad.

Lord Salisbury found the mesmeric Churchill a nuisance; he wryly bracketed him with the premiership, the Foreign Office and the Queen as one of the four great state 'departments' he had to manage. He drew Churchill into the inner circle as Secretary for India in the first short-lived ministry and then as both Chancellor of the Exchequer and Leader of the House in his second administration. It was a meteoric rise for a 37-year-old – but meteors are subject to precipitate descent. Churchill's friendship with Chamberlain and his boldness in proposing domestic measures of a progressive nature marked the beginnings of his ministerial activities, but an early tiff with W H Smith at the War Office over the Army Estimates presaged his spectacular downfall. The Premier refused to overrule Smith and Churchill, thinking himself indispensable, bluffed maladroitly. Barely months into office and he had very publicly resigned. His scintillating powers drained by fatal illness, he died in 1895, all resplendent promise wasted.

Providentially, the very competent W H Smith proved to be an invaluable Leader of the House of Commons, while G J Goschen, an experienced financier, took on the role of Chancellor of the Exchequer with some aplomb. Lord Hartington, whom Lord Salisbury had twice asked if he wished to be prime minister, continued to act as a Liberal Unionist adviser of Whig sympathies, while A J Balfour sprang to the fore as Irish Chief Secretary and resourceful commons debater. Lord Iddesleigh (Stafford Northcote) died abruptly in front of a dismayed Lord Salisbury in 1887, just after the premier had removed him from the Foreign Office.

W H Smith (1825–91) joined his family's bookselling business in 1846. He worked to expand the scope of the enterprise, beginning in 1849 to sell newspapers and books in Britain's railway stations. He later moved into politics, serving in Parliament from 1868 and holding posts as Financial Secretary to the Treasury (1874–7), First Lord of the Admiralty (1877–80), and Secretary for War (1885). He led the House of Commons under Salisbury until his death in 1891, which came as a great personal and political blow to the Prime Minister.

All in all, then, Lord Salisbury emerged from these travails in consummate control of the Conservative government. He was sometimes criticised, especially as the years drew by, for insufficient direction of his colleagues, but his method was to permit ministers a free hand to run their departments without undue interference either from himself or the Cabinet. His close colleague, Sir Michael Hicks Beach, said that Lord Salisbury left his ministers 'very much to themselves unless they consulted him'. The Cabinet met rarely and only for brief sessions during the Salisbury years, while, of course, he managed foreign affairs on much the same individualistic basis. It has rightly been said that he contrived to remove foreign affairs altogether from party considerations, treating the national interest in the superior fashion of a foreign chancellor or, recalling his great ancestor, a Tudor Lord Chancellor.

Lord Salisbury also assisted the landed 'charmed circle' in persisting in political power after their economic power had waned. The perceptive political historian, James Cornford, on whose analytical research we are indebted for a deeper understanding of late Victorian parliamentary life, quotes G C T Barclay, Conservative MP, party agent and founder of the National Penny Bank. He complained to Lord Salisbury in 1898 that, despite all the hard work of many Conservative supporters, places were 'still reserved for the friends and relations of the favoured few'.[3] Apparently Lord Salisbury's promotion of A J Balfour is the origin of the nod-and-a-wink phrase, 'Bob's your uncle'.

Lord Salisbury could scarcely have demurred. Arguing rather speciously that there were no other suitable candidates, he firmly showed preference for his friends and relations, so that, at one point, he involved three nephews, a nephew-in-law, a son-in-law and a son among his ministers. Lord Salisbury earned for his government the epithet of 'the Hotel Cecil'. This was the coinage of the radical MP, Henry Labouchere, with a sly glance at the expensive establishment of that name opened in the 1890s on what originally had been three acres of Cecil land on the Strand, sold for £200,000 by Lord Salisbury in 1888.

On the wider horizon, the 'charmed circle' of the landed gentry remained in control. Two-fifths of Conservative MPs in this era were still of this ilk. They had, as was earlier observed, the advantage of an early start, many of them beginning as young men and gaining sufficient experience to take office at a young age and, with the help of usually safe seats, for long periods. It was different for the self-made commercial, professional and military types, who often came to politics in late middle-age, with membership of Parliament the crowning glory of their careers.

The political position of these land-oriented MPs was, like Lord Salisbury's, an extension of their social position. They shared with Lord Salisbury a concern for agriculture, the church, empire and the armed forces. Apart from flirtations with protection, they were not much removed in economic orthodoxy from the bankers and merchants among their colleagues. Joseph Chamberlain, and his friends, adhered the closer to this group as socialism reared its ugly head and the Unionist appetite for radicalism diminished. The Unionists drew nearer to the Conservatives until eventually the Conservative and Unionist Party emerged in seamless unity. Moreover, a combine of social prejudice and their in-built edge (in respect of their longer parliamentary service and, to be fair, a willingness to take on arduous duties) resulted in governments more heavily weighed toward the landed interest than even the imbalance of its parliamentary representation would have suggested. Twenty-three out of

Henry Du Pré Labouchere (1831–1912) was a radical MP and journalist who had a long and colourful political career. In 1871, he covered the siege of Paris for the *Daily News*, his reports from inside the besieged city making his name. In 1877 he founded the magazine *Truth*. Sitting for Northampton from 1880, he was involved in many *cause célèbres* such as the Parnell trial and the aftermath of the Jameson Raid, but he is perhaps best remembered now for his amendment to the Criminal Law Amendment Act of 1885 which outlawed all male homosexual acts.

the 35 Conservative Cabinet ministers and 38 of the 65 other senior governmental appointments of the 1895/1905 period were from the landed classes.

Lord Salisbury utilised patronage more as a social than a political device, in the sense that, never over enamoured of the joys of power, he was not so much moved by the aim of gathering about him a personal entourage as of ensuring that those he believed to be the right people stayed at the top of society.

In the area of party management, an expanded franchise and the redistribution of seats led to a pertinent alteration in methods of electioneering. The parties had to organise themselves more effectively, with national issues becoming more prominent than the parish pump matters of the old-time 'Eatanswill' kind of election of *Pickwick Papers* fame. Furthermore, as religion lost some of its emotive political appeal, class lines came more to dominate the parliamentary agenda. Both parties had developed more formal central and local arrangements

By 1883 the Conservative National Union, with almost 500 local associations in membership, had become the plaything of Randolph Churchill, seeking a place in the sun with intuitive panache. As its Chairman, he asserted that the Union must 'secure its legitimate influence in the party organisation', a degree of democratisation that Lord Salisbury found appalling. After many recriminations and arguments, Churchill was seduced by the offer of senior office and Hicks Beach became the more benign Chairman of the Union. Salisbury correctly guessed that his rival was *a sham alternative*; he dragged the crutch of the National Union from under his arm; the struggle as to whether the Conservative Party should be a popular or an authoritarian organisation was over, and the Union was, in Winston Churchill's words, 'peacefully laid to rest.' The ruthless Aretas Akers-Douglas became Chief Whip and the hard-working Captain R W E Middleton became national party agent and Secretary of the Union. Every local Conservative association was automatically affiliated to the national body and a format of ten provincial groups was put in place. The rank and file, frightened by the 1880 electoral debacle but now relieved by Lord Salisbury's composed leadership, was complacent. From fund-raising to sophisticated canvassing, from the employment of socially attractive aristocratic whips to the wooing of the press, nothing was left to chance by these two excellent organisers and their several keen lieutenants. The threesome – Salisbury, Akers-Douglas and Middleton – formed 'a remarkable trium-virate' that guaranteed the parliamentary and membership sections worked in near perfect unison.

A curiosity of Victorian politics was that both great parties suffered self-destruction and re-emergence as coalitions. The Tory Peelite wing had shored up the Liberal Party and, later, the up-and-coming Lib-Lab representatives would back the briefly resurgent Edwardian Liberals. In between whiles the Liberal Party split over Irish Home Rule; as we have observed, only the Liberal Unionist segment kept the Conservatives in government. It must again be emphasised that it was Lord Salisbury's careful massaging of this alliance that kept it in being; and there were other benefits – it was the presence of many Liberal Unionists in urban constituencies that first eased the Conservative Party more comfortably into the onetime Liberal industrial towns and cities of England.

There was an additional component. This was the Primrose League. Named after Disraeli's allegedly favourite flower, it was formed in 1883, non-coincidentally the year when the Corrupt Practices Act made bribery and sumptuous expend-iture at elections illicit. The parties now needed hordes of unpaid volunteers to do the canvassing, the knocking-up of voters and all the other jobs necessary for polling in a modernised democracy. Originally an adjunct of Randolph Churchill's 'Tory Democracy' scheme, it became the volunteer army of Lord Salisbury's Conservative Party. It was all-embracing, with countesses rubbing shoulders with starry-eyed working people, and with a programme of social gaiety – bazaars, fêtes, lantern-slide shows – that was new to British politics. It was its very vulgarity, according to the enthusiastic Lady Salisbury, that ensured its success. It peaked at a million members in 1910, one of the largest voluntary political bodies ever recruited; it proved to be an essential asset to the party propaganda and electoral machine.

Educated men do not like going round, hat in hand, begging for votes of a mob (that) require him to swallow the most claptrap pledges as a condition for their support.

SALISBURY

It was one of the first opportunities afforded women to break into party politics and here Lord Salisbury was as astute as ever. Never a hearty, bucolic sort of Tory landlord, he recognised that women might temper what he saw as the repulsive nastiness of the male of the species. He was not so opposed to female suffrage as might have been expected. It is sometimes forgotten that women did already have a vote in other than national elections. By the end of the century many thousands of women could vote in municipal, county and school board elections on the same property bases as applied, at that point, to 75 per cent of the male population. Women had been elected to the first school boards in 1870 and as poor law guardians in 1873; two women, after a legal tussle, were elected to the founding London County Council of 1889, while a clarifying act allowing women to sit on all local government councils was passed in 1907.

Lord Salisbury did not see as much to fear in women politicians and voters as did the huge majority of Victorian males. Most men adhered to the current dogma of the 'private' and 'public' spheres as gender-specific, with the domestic female role complementing the male bread-winning, professional one. Voting and politicking fell into that latter camp. Judging by the post-suffrage right-wing activities of Emmeline and Christabel, if not Sylvia, Pankhurst, to say nothing of voting patterns until deep into the 20th century, Lord Salisbury was probably right in his assessment that the Conservatives had less to fear than progressive politicians from the female franchise.

It was not that Lord Salisbury, unlike his hostess wife, enjoyed the social aspect of politics. *Educated men*, he opined, *do not like going round, hat in hand, begging for votes of a mob (that) require him to swallow the most claptrap pledges as a condition for their support.* He rued the day when *two day-labourers shall outvote Rothschild.*[4] Yet disdain was not the same as disregard. He accepted the situation and attempted, with much advantage, to steer democracy in a right–wing direction.

There were other strings to the Conservative bow and one of them was the monarchy. The English republican movement reached a peak about 1870, only to be forgotten as, by the

Sir Charles Wentworth Dilke (1843–1911) was a Liberal politician whose promising career was cut short by scandal. On the radical wing of the party, he was an ally of Joseph Chamberlain in Gladstone's 1880–5 government, and as president of the local government board seemed set for higher office. But involvement in a scandalous divorce case in 1885–6 meant he never held office again, although he returned to Parliament in the 1890s and was even touted as a possible leader of the Independent Labour Party.

end of the century, royalism bordered on adulation. Queen Victoria's brooding withdrawal after the death of the Prince Consort in 1861, coupled with the vast expenditure engendered by her several offspring, among them an extravagant Prince of Wales, fuelled the republican fires. It was not solely a working class drive, for its focus was Sir Charles Dilke, the radical young Liberal baronet and minister, destined, some thought, to be a Liberal party leader, but felled by a divorce scandal.

The movement was not of epic proportions but it was serious enough, and, in the wake of Disraeli's clever wooing of the Queen, Lord Salisbury acknowledged that a popular monarchy, especially one wedded inexorably to the landed interest and the aristocracy, tended to favour Conservatism. He found Queen Victoria, as a person, limited, although, as both aged, their relationship considerably mellowed. Perhaps the head of the long established Cecil household regarded the German royals as 'Johans-come-lately'. He was also shrewd enough to spot how uncannily the Queen and her respectable middle-class and aspiring working-class subjects saw eye to eye, and he discreetly used her as a pulse of public opinion.

Much as he disliked pomp and circumstance, he did not stand in the way of the late Victorian augmentation of monarchical pageantry. The mock-medieval titles and livery that attended the Jubilees and other ceremonies, and which still offer their splendid colourful allure to tourists, rubber-neckers and monarchists today, were largely the invention of the late 19th century. Something of a pseudo-religious sentiment attended the deepening affection for Queen Victoria, an emotion missing from royalist attachment since 'Good King Charles' golden days.'

It fitted well with Lord Salisbury's belief in the hierarchical state and Queen Victoria acted as a much-loved talisman, particularly when national prestige, in war or in Empire, those definitively Conservative issues, was imperilled. It also fitted well with what has been called 'the medieval dream', that chaste late Victorian love of a fanciful rural past and guilt about the inroads of a noisome industrialism. Eric Hobsbawm has written that 'the characteristical mythical Britain of the travel poster ... the heavy incrustation of British life with pseudo-medieval and other rituals, like the cult of monarchy, dates back [only] to the late Victorian period, as does the pretence that the Englishman is a thatched-cottager or a country squire at heart'.

It began years before with Disraeli's 'Young England' movement. It is a proclivity that may be noted in the architecture – the 'vibrant medievalism' of Augustus Pugin; the mock-Gothic Houses of Parliament or St Pancras Station – in an affection for the historical novels of Sir Walter Scott and his successors, like Charles Reade and Charles Kingsley; in the wave of delight in Arthurian chivalry and 'folklore', the very word a Victorian coinage; in the 'urban folk-ballad operas' of Gilbert and Sullivan; in the attempts of the revered Victorian constitutional scholars, like William Stubbs and E W Maitland, to track down legal and institutional origins in early medieval times; in the English love-affair with the garden, with the trim lawn – 'the handkerchief of the Lord', according to Walt Whitman – and with the Capability Brown sort of municipal park, aping the 18th-century rolling estate, and many, many other examples.

Although the radicals had their 'Norman Yoke' theory about the loss of Anglo-Saxon freedoms after the Conquest and although Robert Blatchford's left-wing tale, published in 1893/4 with the significant title of *Merrie England*, sold 750,000 copies, the mood favoured the forces of Conservatism. Shuddering inwardly at the tastelessness of it all, Lord

Salisbury clenched his cultural teeth and became the Masonic-sounding Grand Master of the Primrose League in 1884. The Primrose League was suffused in medievalist imagery. It had 'habitations', such as the King Athelstan 'habitation' at Malmesbury, and 'tributes', a modest threepence a year, where simpler souls made do with branches and subscriptions.

It would not be long before, in the years before the First World War, Robert Baden-Powell, the hero of Mafeking, would be adopting a pseudo-sylvan back-to-nature styling and nomenclature for the highly successful Boy Scout movement. It is of passing interest that, as Andrew Roberts reminds us, Baden-Powell modelled his format on the Mafeking Cadet Corps or 'Scouts', aged nine to 15, which was organised by Lord Salisbury's son, Edward, a major in the Grenadier Guards and Baden-Powell's chief of staff.

Another institution, this time of genuine vintage, that Lord Salisbury deployed on behalf of Conservatism was the House of Lords. In fact, he rescued it from its mid-century somnolence and crafted from it if not a sharp rapier then a blunt instrument. *The nation is our master*, declaimed Lord Salisbury, ... *the House of Commons is not*. That appeal over the heads of the representatives, rather like the joining of hands with the monarchy, was a deliberate Conservative wedge. It was a *rash inference* on the part of the commons to assume they knew the changing will of the people over a six-year period of changing events. It was the lords' task to defend the people against such presumption. Lord Salisbury made the most of his own presence in the Lords, following a period when, in the main, the dominant premiers, like Peel, Gladstone and Disraeli, had chiefly served in the Commons.

> *The nation is our master ... the House of Commons is not.*
>
> SALISBURY

He assiduously rebuilt the strength and reputation of the House of Lords, even as he furnished it with a predominant Tory majority. It was largely through his endeavours that the membership of the upper house rose from 372 in 1830 to 562 in 1900; in the two Jubilee years of 1887 and 1897 he created almost a thousand peers, privy councillors, baronets and knights, the majority of them of Conservative persuasion. Lord Salisbury thought that the noble house was *a paradise of bores*,[5] but then he tended to dislike most of the agencies he believed to be essential to a static society. It certainly did not deter him from constructing yet another barrier against progress. Nor was he any more sentimental about this than he was about the monarchy. In 1898 he even contemplated the possibility of life peers as a further reinforcement of the barrier.

Nor was Lord Salisbury polite about his fellow landowners. In 1851 he wrote, in the hard-hitting journalistic style he later preferred not to recall, of *the dwarfed, languid, nerveless, emasculated dilettantism of the higher classes*. This never stopped him from defending the precept of property. He wrote that *every community has natural leaders, to whom, if they are not misled by the insane passion for equality, they will instinctively defer*. Their attributes were often birth, intellectual power and culture, the leisure to prepare for their duties without *the taint of greed*, and the class discipline of honour. These were the optional traits of the elite; one other was indispensable – there was *always wealth*.[6]

Thus Lord Salisbury had no hesitation, unlike some Tory backwoodsmen, in welcoming new money to the elitist feast. He recognised that 'urban property' was becoming as critical an element as rural landowning. Hugh Lupus Grosvenor became the first Duke of Westminster in 1874, without any of the conventional regal connection that usually prompted ducal status, on the basis of metropolitan landlordship. He was the richest man in Britain and his descendants remain today among the wealthiest landlords in the nation. The influx of shipping, brewing and other commercial monies meant that, in 1901, there were 298 estates valued at over £100,000, compared with but 68 in 1858. The super-rich merchant class of millionaires – there were 31 in Britain in 1900 – were attracted to the Tories; the Rothschild family moved to Conservatism in the 1880s.

Land was still important. A third of the land was in upper-class hands and, despite its decline in the economic stakes, it remained politically influential, not least because industrial wealth bought into it. That very busy and able politician, W H Smith, invested in a 5,000-acre estate in Suffolk in 1877 and made good his credentials as country squire, having made his fortune as a newsagent and bookseller. Lord Salisbury worked assiduously to incorporate the plutocracy and the aristocracy, acknowledging that wealth, not land, was the key. It is true that, like his fellow aristocrats, he despised the 'rich vulgarians' and 'billiard marker gentry', as the new rich were sometimes described. He would have agreed with Dorothy Parker's dictum that 'if you want to know what God thinks of money, look at the people he gave it to'. But, politically, he embraced hardworking and self-made men like Chamberlain, Smith and R A Cross, barrister and banker and a capable member of both Disraeli and Salisbury Cabinets. Beyond that, he was responsible for securing the loyal allegiance as well as the bustling contribution of the business interest by his elevation of many of them to the peerage. In the ten years before 1886 only four men from a commercial background had been ennobled; between 1886 and 1914 70 of the 200 new peers represented the industrial and business community.

Much has been made of the 'embourgoisement of the proletariat', that right-wing seduction of the respectable artisan class by the temptation of upward social mobility and the xenophobic allure of martial patriotism. Less perhaps has been heard of what might be crudely called 'the aristocratisation of the bourgeoisie'. Lord Salisbury's ennoblement of railway directors was the peak of this tendency for the upper middle class, in the style of Galsworthy's Forsytes, to adopt the manners of their perceived superiors. Richard Cobden, most clear-sighted of the mid-century radicals, observed the origins of this trend with disgust. His ideal had been that free trade would be the prerequisite of peaceful relations among the developed nations. The developing regions would be thus unfettered by political control, as part of that same trading idyll. In consequence, he believed that the armed forces could be reduced and taxes cut, albeit with spare funds transferred to laudable ends such as secular education. 'A nation which undertakes to sway the destinies of Europe by bullying one half and protecting the other must,' he said, 'make up its mind to bear the expense.' He believed, with some accuracy, that the army and navy officer cadres were 'mere extensions of the aristocracy's pension list'.

He was frustrated and distressed by what happened. The Whig wing of the Liberal Party swamped the Manchester radicals and the industrial magnates jostled to join the upper classes, forming what the Germans were, in their own case, to call the '*Schlottjunkertum*', a 'chimney aristocracy'. 'The middle class has been content with the very crumbs from their table', said Cobden ruefully, as his erstwhile colleagues adopted patrician ways, waxed bellicose about England abroad, sent their children to public schools and sat on the county benches as high sheriffs. In a picturesque illustration, he harangued the Manchester council for adopting the junketing, regalia and livery of the antiquated London Corporation. Blasted was his dream of Manchester becoming a present-day Athens; once their champion, he dismissed Mancunian businessmen as 'glorying in being the toadies of a clodpole aristocracy'.

A vivid personification of this change may be found in the life of A N Hornby (1847–1929), the Lancashire and England cricket captain. The child of a successful Blackburn textile family, he went to Harrow and, fleetingly, to Oxford, before some involvement in the family business and, more substantively, a career of all-round sporting splendour, living off its proceeds. He resided in the plush meadows of Cheshire at Parkfield, Nantwich, with its country-house cricket ground and its stable of prancing hunters, while he was a captain in the East Cheshire Militia and fearlessly took on rowdies in both Manchester and Australian cricket crowds. The Manchester man had become the Lancashire gentleman. The evocative cricket writer, Neville Cardus, entitled him 'the Squire of Lancashire'.

Lord Salisbury did not, of course, create these phenomena of adoration of the monarchy and glorification of the aristocracy. He was, however, very alert to their power and how they mattered in the political fray. It was not long, for instance, before leading Conservatives and Salisbury acolytes began to fly the blue banner as candidates in city suburbs and industrial towns, among them his close kin Gerald Balfour in Leeds Central, Lord Cranborne in Darwen, Lancashire, and Arthur Balfour in East Manchester (where he also became a vice-president of Newton Heath football club, the precursors of Manchester United, thereby reaching, for many admirers of that triumphant team, the apex of his career). The Hotel Cecil was keen to be seen as the party of the business and professional classes and the champions of so-called Villa Toryism.

The motors for recruiting working-class Tory voters were

deference, Jingoism and the desire for respectability, with organisations like the Primrose League geared up to encourage such feelings. Violence in Ireland drove many middle class Liberals into the Conservative camp and this also applied to some artisan electors. Religion still played some part, with a detestation of Roman Catholicism coupled with that anti-Irish feeling. 'You are a catholic, sir,' a lady railway passenger is recorded as having said to the architect, Augustus Pugin, in these years; 'guard, let me out – I must get into another carriage.' This reactive Protestant mood was equally to be found in working-class districts of Liverpool and elsewhere and was a solid foundation for Tory advances in such areas.

A further ace in the Tory hand was the promotion of an unbridled life-style of 'beer and bonhomie', with, for instance, a flexible attitude to the licensing laws. This also won the plaudits of the brewers, often the generous sponsors of Conservative campaigns. This was in plain conflict with the 'moral faddism' of the Liberals, with their puritanical Dissenting views on temperance, anti-gaming and the like. Yet another interesting issue was the effect of the secret ballot, usually viewed as a protection for employees and tenants against the oppression of employers and landlords. It has been suggested that, in the later decades of the 19th century, it also eased the voting path of those afraid of peer groups, such as fellow trades unionists, allowing working men to vote Tory with impunity.

James Cornford has argued that, in rural areas, 'dominance', not deference, is the precise word, in that the support was 'exacted'. He points to the disruption of agricultural trades unionism by eviction and blacklisting, by the refusal to allow village or church halls to be used for meetings and by the sheer close personal involvement of the farming process. There were tiny handfuls of labourers, often linked to farmers by tenancies, under constant watch, very different to the concentrated communities of, say, miners or cotton workers. The Conservative MPs in the countryside were also closely wedded to the locality: 50 per cent of them lived in the constituency and owned property there, while many had family connections in the vicinity. It all added up to a considerable advantage for the Conservatives.

Another tactic used during the Salisbury years was the drag on registration of voters. It was a cumbersome and archaic process, with, for instance, the 12 months' residential qualifying period telling against manual workers often faced with constant changes of job and workplace. It has been estimated that as a many as a million men were disenfranchised in any one year because of this stratagem; and this at a time when businessmen and graduates had plural votes, usually Conservative, amounting to some 7 per cent of the total electorate.

The Tories had been concerned by the sudden rise after 1884 of the countryside voting power from about 900,000 to 2.5 million and, as noted earlier, Lord Salisbury strove mightily to engineer a redistribution of constituency strengths that benefited his party. In so doing, incidentally, he again showed his unfeeling lack of nostalgia. The slicing up of well-established boroughs and counties destroyed some of the organic structure of parliamentary representation, the forerunner of the aimlessly non-organic if mathematically satisfying seats of today, which frequently bear no relation to the geographic or local governmental perceptions of the residents.

Not content with gerrymandering the vote, Lord Salisbury and his advisers were eager to manipulate the voters. Up to 40 per cent of men did not vote between 1885 and 1918. Domestic servants, policemen, soldiers in barracks, and those on poor relief were expressly excluded, as well as those thousands who found it difficult to register. In the countryside, where a Liberal backlash of the rural proletariat was feared, the Salisbury target was to keep the registrations down below the 60 per cent mark; this was deemed to be manageable. The choice of election days during harvest time, when labourers could be ill spared to conduct their democratic rights, was an additional shot in the Tory constitutional locker. Lord Salisbury was fundamentally opposed to the concept of *those who lived in hovels ... holding political power*. He worried that full-blown democracy would demolish all that he held good and sacred. Lord Salisbury maybe overestimated the power of the franchise, but he did his best to make sure that its power was neutralised as far as was possible. The Conservative leader, in all these ways, ensured that his Tory precepts informed every branch of governmental operation.

This concludes the analysis of Lord Salisbury's work as Prime Minister in the foreign, domestic and political fields. His health, never really sound, worsened after 1898. In 1899, his closest ally and mainstay, his much-loved wife, died after a long illness. Understandably, he was stricken with grief. He finally resigned as Prime Minister in July 1902, his nephew, Arthur Balfour, taking over the management of the 'Hotel Cecil'. Lord Salisbury did not long survive the Queen who had come to regard highly the last of her many prime ministers. Broken in body and spirit, he died at Hatfield House on 22 August 1903 at the age of 73.

Part Three

THE LEGACY

Chapter 7: The Shorter-Term Consequences

I cannot help thinking that in discussions of this kind, a great deal of misapprehension arises from the popular use of maps on a small scale ... If the noble lord would use a large map – say one on the scale of the Ordnance Map of England – he would find that the distance between Russia and India is not to be measured by the finger and thumb, but by a rule.[1]

As Lord Salisbury's strength and authority waned, so did his government founder a little. The South African War, although resulting in victory, had been a blow. The diplomacy had failed; the expense had been great; the army had, initially, faltered; the conclusion had been disastrously untidy. What was called 'national efficiency' had been wanting. Recruitment had revealed widespread ill-health among the working classes: 40 per cent of those volunteering for service in the Boer War had been rejected on medical grounds, a sobering thought about the industrial as well as the military resources of a nation faced with both commercial and martial competition.

Fiscal rectitude of the Gladstonian brand had weakened in a shift from orthodoxy with what were called 'knaves' tinkering with currency, tariffs and what-not. There was less emphasis on sound finances and balanced budgets. The upshot was that central public expenditure leapt from £93 million in 1870,

9 per cent of gross national product (GNP), to £200 million, 25 per cent of GNP, in 1900. Defence, in particular, but also education and public health expenditure had risen significantly, with much more money conveyed as grants-in-aid to local government. Lord Salisbury disliked much of this.

The 1900 'Khaki' election had been won by the Conservative/Unionist coalition in a weary mood of negativity and relief, helped by the fact that the still disorganised Liberals had not fought in 300 constituencies. Lord Salisbury's nephew, Arthur Balfour, inherited a rocky political construct that soon collapsed. The Liberals, fortified by rapidly improved organisation and with a spring in their step, came triumphantly to power in 1906. The Salisbury era was well and truly over.

There is some controversy as to whether the busy Asquith administration was the last fling of 19th-century Gladstonian Liberalism or the first flush of 20th-century left-wing Collectivism. Either way, it was quite incisive, with social reforms that would have horrified Lord Salisbury and a successfully bold challenge to the House of Lords that would have enraged him. Moreover, behind the spacious composure often associated with Edwardian Britain there were seething instances of rebellious and violent protest. There were savage labour disputes, militant suffragette agitation and ferocious Irish disturbances. Indeed, some historians have surmised that, had not the 1914–18 war intervened, Great Britain might have undergone revolution on a fundamental scale.

Mounting war scares and crises led to that dreadful conflict, its original Balkan focus indicative that the old Eastern Question was again to the fore. Although the war was dominated in English minds by the horrors of the Western front, it had been largely 'Eastern' considerations that had caused Britain to consider participation. R K Ensor wrote that the Treaty of Berlin, negotiated by Lord Salisbury with

Disraeli in 1878, by its 'damning of the Russian current had results not foreseen in 1878. In a profounder sense than Bosnia-Herzegovina or Macedonia it caused the 1914 War'. Moreover, in consequence of the German-Russian rift and Austro-German alliance dating from that treaty, there emerged 'the grouping from which the World War resulted.' It is difficult, of course, to disentangle Lord Salisbury's own contribution from this long cycle of events and incidents. Indeed, his calm statecraft might, had he survived, have helped a little in foreign affairs during this uneasy phase.

The bulk of Lord Salisbury's policies were about deferment. It might be urged that, by providing a spatchcock solution to the Eastern Question in the 1870s, he postponed hostilities for over a generation. On the other hand, it might be asserted that, because the solution was something of a patchwork quilt, it could not be enduring and made war more probable. It is a difficult call. British Rail managers used to complain that, if they announced in Spring that fares would be held stable until the New Year, the banner headlines would scream 'rail fares to increase in January'. Lord Salisbury's long reign over British diplomacy is subject to the same ambivalence of assessment. An allied issue for a consciously obstruction-ist statesman like Lord Salisbury is whether or not delaying tactics have the effect of storing up trouble. It could be that deferred surgery has of necessity to be more heroic and hazardous. Were, then, the pre-1914 social problems at home and the Irish upheavals, to say nothing of the tragedy of the First World War, the worse in character because, deliberately, nothing had been done for 20 years? And thus was 'progress' the more advanced or drastic for arriving later?

Another gloss on this theory is that a period of calm after the furore of radical change offers a chance for consolidation. In that scenario the inter-war years accord a respite after the

The changing role of the prime minister

It would be wrong to imagine that, except on rare occasions, First Lords of the Treasury have the time or the inclination to reflect upon the degree to which the topology of the Premiership is changing around them. As Gladstone, writing as Prime Minister, noted in his diary on the last day of 1868, 'Swimming for his life, a man does not see much of the country through which the river winds.' We can identify [however] chairing the Cabinet, dealing with the Monarch and managing Parliament, as one of the core functions of the early premiership. Another is responsibility for warfare. It is significant that the 1950s Cabinet Office file on 'The Constitutional System' refers to a body created in either 1620 or 1621 as 'A Standing Council for War'. 'Probably a committee of the Privy Council', it notes, without quite declaring it to be the prototypical 'War Cabinet'. We need to move on another 60 years from Walpole's appointment as First Lord to find the next rash of historical accretions which begin to develop a kind of doctrine of prime ministerial indispensability. They came in a cluster in the early 1780s and finish with Churchill establishing the primacy of the premier over nuclear weapons policy in the 1940s... . Although war had long been a central concern of the Privy Council, it was the Napoleonic Wars at the turn of the 18th to the 19th century which demonstrated that warfare had become an intensely prime ministerial function. Henceforth, war was added to money (it is important not to forget the importance of the Prime Minister as First Lord of the Treasury; Mrs Thatcher did not) as a great enhancer of the relative power of the Prime Minister. Not until the Hartington Commission of 1889 were serious steps taken to plan for a substantial reshaping of government in time of war. Yet so poorly did Whitehall adapt to the demands of the Boer War that the then Prime Minister, the Marquess of Salisbury, was moved to admit to the House of Lords in 1900 that he did *not believe in the perfection of the British Constitution as an instrument for war*. Only the creation of the Committee of Imperial Defence by Balfour in 1904 did matters seriously improve. [Peter Hennessy: *The Prime Minister* (Penguin Books, London: 2000) p 44ff] vibrant days of Edwardian Liberalism, while the 'Butskellite' quarter-century after 1951 provided a similar restorative after Clement Attlee's 'silent revolution'. Thus 20 years or so of Lord Salisbury's ministries may be seen as a settling in time for the dramatic shifts of Gladstone's first administration. It was at the end of that ebullient phase of parliamentary activity in 1874 that Disraeli described the Liberal front bench as 'a row of exhausted volcanoes'. It was part compliment and part insult. The volcanoes had erupted with some heat; now they were extinguished and dormant. It was perhaps time for an interval of consolidation. Of course, there are many arguments about such assessments. For example, David Thompson dismisses the 1920s and 1930s as an era of 'incorrigible immobilisme', with politicians and people alike sunk in inertia, introspection and torpor, while other historians see signs of creative energy in one or other of these periods of post-radical somnolence.

Lord Salisbury was a Conservative with a capital 'C'. He preserved but yet did not often backtrack. He was pessimistic enough about the levers of government to believe that, if reactionary legislation was tried, it might prove in practice detrimental to his cause. He loathed the Prussian *despotism of officials* and saw little use in bureaucratic action. He attempted, then, to hold the line exactly where it was at that particular moment and to shore up the barricade as stalwartly as he could. It is a depressing kind of politics. Lord Salisbury recognised the inevitability of the change he detested. He knew it was difficult to put back the clock. He was resolved to stop it if possible, and, when that was no longer possible, to slow it down. But, day by day, year by year, there could only be, as with his clear intellect he must have recognised, eventual disappointment.

There is a strange twist to the plot. The Conservative

Party, stunned by reverse after reverse in the pre-1914 years, and with the House of Lords in disarray, looked to be reeling. Ewen Green argues that, whilst the conventional wisdom suggests that the Liberal party never recovered from the First World War, the complementary and perhaps more significant truth is that, without the interference of the war, the Conservative party might have been obliterated altogether. Left-wing enthusiasts might echo the key phrase uttered by Marlow, the narrator in Joseph Conrad's *Lord Jim* – 'what a chance missed … '.

While the 1914–18 war gave rise to all manner of upheavals elsewhere, it appears that in Great Britain it had the effect of quietening the pre-1914 social tumult and averting wholesale change, including the demise of the Tory party that Lord Salisbury had worked so tirelessly to mould. In this interpretation, the Great War was an ill wind that, contrary to proverbial belief, blew no good for anyone. It is true that the death of the Conservative Party, like the death of pantomime, has been wrongly prophesied on more than one occasion. Both have survived by the same astute expedient of recruiting modish elements by way of recuperation.

In the purist sense, there was hardly a pristine Conservative government for 100 years after the repeal of the Corn Laws. Lord Salisbury's 'virtual coalition' with the Liberal Unionists was the beginning of a lengthy period when, apart from the Liberal ministries of the 1900s, the Conservatives dominated British politics through a series of strategic alliances. There were wartime coalitions and peacetime 'national' governments that allowed Lord Salisbury's party to rule the roost until 1945. Because of this there is something of a myth about the impact of the two-party system during those 100 years, despite Private Willis' assertion in *Iolanthe* that 'every boy and every gal that's born into the world alive is either a little Liberal or else a little Conservative.' In fact, the period after 1945 offers a much more straightforward demonstration of that phenomenon. Sixty years have elapsed with only an occasional murmur of alliance or coalition. The clear-cut party score line – Conservatives 35 years; Labour 25 years – is itself a moderately decent account of the end-to-end play of the party game.

It makes for a curious mix. The route to 1914 from 1878 might look, in retrospect, inevitable, but any pathway through the Balkans story is strewn with pitfalls and false trails. It would be unwise to find too much blood on Lord Salisbury's hands. However, in so far as the Congress of Berlin did lead to Sarajevo, then Lord Salisbury might take some indirect credit, if Ewen Green is at all correct, for the survival and eminence of the Conservative party after the 1914–18 War.

As for that other important cog in the Salisbury wheel – the imperial component – that, too, raises questions. With much of North America lost in 1783, but with major bases in India, the West Indies, Canada and Australasia, the British Empire underwent a great African and Asian expansion during Lord Salisbury's time. However, as Empires go, the British Empire went fairly quickly. Given that it peaked about 1890, then, in an average lifetime, it had all but vanished. The former colonies fought for and won their independence, with, if at times grudgingly, the agreement and help of the imperial power. Despite the Commonwealth linkage, many ex-imperial units went their own way. That made for a remarkably short-lived Empire, compared with the Roman precedent, or the enormous longevity of several ancient Empires. Lord Salisbury would have especially mourned the loss of India, as he would have that of Ireland, although the despotic antics of some of the liberated colonies, no less the periodic Irish troubles since 1916, would probably have caused him to pass sardonic comment.

The 1914–18 War; the Irish republic; colonial independence; major social reform – it does appear that in the very fields where he had concentrated so much of his manifold delaying powers, Lord Salisbury suffered set-backs in the historical short-term. Nonetheless, to his depressive and pessimistic mind, the years of stalling before these events befell might have given him cause for some gloomy satisfaction. Anthony Trollope's famous quotation from *Phineas Redux* (1874) has some relevance. 'It is the necessary nature of a political party in this country to avoid, as long as it can be avoided, the consideration of any question which involves a great change. There is a consciousness on the minds of leading politicians that the pressure from behind, forcing upon them great measures, drives them almost quicker than they can go, so that it becomes a necessity with them to resist rather than to aid the pressure which will certainly be at last effective by its own strength. The best carriage-horses are those which can most steadily hold back against the coach as it trundles down the hill.' Lord Salisbury was the best carriage-horse on the political hill.

Chapter 8: The Longer-Term Legacies

No lesson seems to be so deeply inculcated by the experience of life as that you should never trust experts. If you believe the doctors, nothing is wholesome: if you believe the theologians, nothing is innocent: if you believe the soldiers, nothing is safe. They all require to have strong wine diluted by a very large admixture of insipid common sense.[1]

Why, given a longish period in the historical doldrums, has Lord Salisbury recently been the subject of excited interest and attempted rehabilitation? Since his daughter's rather heavy going biography, published after the First World War, and one or two other rather neutral studies, there had been little novel on the theme of Lord Salisbury until quite recently. Then, in the last few years, there has been a minor flurry of texts. Among these have been works, for instance, by David Steele, Michael Bentley and, most tellingly, Andrew Roberts. Their claim, overt and covert, is that Lord Salisbury is ripe for rediscovery and for a place alongside Gladstone and Disraeli as the third titanic statesman of the last half of the 19th century.

The suddenness and the comprehensive nature of this, to deploy a televisual term, makeover is remarkable. It may

No lesson seems to be so deeply inculcated by the experience of life as that you should never trust experts.

· SALISBURY

possibly be explained by the intertwining of two factors. The first is 'the pendulum of revisionism'. Although it is true in the case of Lord Salisbury, as for other historical characters, that hitherto hidden evidence comes to light in fustian journals and dusty archives, there is also the desire to provide a more balanced or quite contrary view of the original estimate. It is the natural reaction of the historian as storyteller. The latest commentary on the nefarious murderer, Hawley Harvey Crippen, hanged in 1910, suggests he was innocent; there would be little mileage in proving yet again that he was guilty. The Kennedy assassination industry has swung from the lone gunman conclusion, through a bewildering web of tangled conspiracies – and has now swung back to the solitary killer explanation. Richard III, it is now proclaimed, was not such a 'bad king' as Sellar and Yeatman decreed in *1066 and All That*. Next year we may find that Alfred the Great was not so great. It was, then, time for Lord Salisbury to have a good press for a change.

But why should it be this particular focus? This is possibly where the second factor comes into play. As the historian E H Carr and others have sought to explain, in history there are not only the facts but also the 'interpreter', with much the same jumble of data kaleidoscopically revealing a different picture as the mix is shaken by another hand. The lens alters according to the values and mores of the hour; to take an obvious example, Lord Salisbury's racism, not regarded as untoward in his day, would now be regarded as abhorrent.

A substantial amount of history written over the last two or three generations had been penned by scholars predominantly liberal to Marxist in taste, as befitted the political and intellectual culture in which they lived and worked. Robert Ensor, a leading critic of Lord Salisbury, whom he regarded as second-rate abroad and indolent at home, wrote from a left of centre, maybe Fabian, perspective. In his magisterial volume in the classic *Oxford History of England* series – as Andrew Roberts feelingly reminds – he did much to push Lord Salisbury on to the back benches of history for myriads of history students.

It is understandable, and invigorating, that, as Britain swung in the 1960s and especially after the spectacular oil-related inflation of 1973/4 to a less collectivist and more individualistic mood, the focus of historical scholarship switched accordingly. In a more materialistic, xenophobic and pugnacious world, with an accent, commonly associated with the premiership of Margaret Thatcher, on self rather than a supposedly non-existent society, a right-wing vein of historical interpretation challenged the previous left-wing bias. It is a school of thinking often identified with the brilliantly persuasive Cambridge historian, Maurice Cowling (1926–2005). Interestingly, he helped found the Salisbury Group in 1978. This was a high Tory and highly intellectual sect of which Lord Salisbury would have approved but which was perhaps too arcane to become widely known, another of its traits of which its eponymous hero would have been proud. The bustling revisionism of this phase of historical writing supplied compelling justifications of capitalist entrepreneurship and imperial expansion, whilst even the 1914–18 War was recast with unavoidable losses and efficient generals. The *laissez-faire* doctrine was revitalised and the staid mean-spirited bureaucracy of the collectivist state was denigrated.

Of course – as these scholarly modern analyses of Lord Salisbury exemplify – it is light and shade, not black and white. It is fascinating to observe how different historians look at Lord Salisbury from different angles, some seeing foibles where others see virtues. At the extreme, Andrew Roberts looked at what Lord Salisbury did and nodded approval, where

Robert Ensor sniffed disparagingly. It is fair to say that, with the availability of new material, the modern biographies of Lord Salisbury – and here again Andrew Roberts provides an evocative example – paint a richer portrait of the Tory marquess. This especially applies to his private life, where one is relieved to find, after the brutishness of his childhood and youth, Lord Salisbury relaxed and mordantly amusing amidst his family. It makes for a more three-dimensional study.

Politically, nonetheless, there are contrasting views of Lord Salisbury, about which, of course, it is ultimately the task of the student to decide. As for the Salisburyan legacy, on the face of it the longer-term version seems no more fruitful than the shorter-term heritage. Society is obviously much changed in many ways from the Salisbury epoch and, for instance, he would have frowned upon what David Lloyd George prophetically called the 'morbid footballism' of the masses.

But wait … if one looks at the Britain of today against the pattern that a Victorian radical, such as Richard Cobden, might hopefully have anticipated, then Lord Salisbury's stalling of change might appear to have had some patently substantive results. First of all there is the survival of the Conservative Party itself, a political force widely regarded, in the last half of the 20th century and until its recent temporary collapse, as one of the most formidably organised of such groups in Western Europe. Next there are a number of social and cultural stoppers that Lord Salisbury helped to lay against the opening door of progress and which are still, one way or another, in stubborn place.

One of Lord Salisbury's chief anxieties was that political democracy would become equated with economic democracy. Far from that happening, the degree of inequality in the country is still extremely high, with, sadly, profoundly vicious effects on social determinants, like health, crime and educational outcomes. The recent research of Richard Wilkinson suggests that 'poorer countries with fairer wealth distribution are healthier and happier than richer more unequal nations'. Lord Salisbury's adroit equipoise of a landed-cum-mercantile plutocracy has been sustained. The cant slogan of 'equality of opportunity' has been peddled as a substitute for real social justice and 'meritocracy' (coined, ironically enough, as a derisory value by the social entrepreneur, Michael Young) has become a virtuous aim. Lord Salisbury would have rejoiced to observe that, in his phrase, *always wealth* remains the motor of a hierarchical society.

Andrew Roberts wrote a pamphlet for the Libertarian Alliance in 1999 in which he scintillatingly developed the theme of Lord Salisbury as an advocate of libertarianism and a foe of state intercession. This publication bears the motto of the Alliance on its masthead; to wit, 'For Life, Liberty and Property'. 'Life' is an unexceptional ideal, while 'liberty', with certain riders, is certainly acceptable – it is 'property' that is the giveaway. The slogan appears to entertain the idea that the state should abjure from interfering with private property, *as presently distributed*. That assuredly echoes Lord Salisbury's static view of the subject. The fact that the state might have interfered in the past to procure the property for the owner is conveniently forgotten. An old tale usefully illustrates the dilemma. A tramp was discovered trespassing on the grounds of a large estate by its wealthy owner. The tramp was ordered off and an altercation ensued, during which the landlord exclaimed. 'I'll have you know my ancestors fought for this land.' The tramp began to remove his ragged coat. 'Alright then,' he announced, 'I'll fight you for it.' It could have been Lord Salisbury, recalling how his forebear, David Cecil, was gifted a parcel of land by the state, in the royal name of Henry VII, having fortuitously fought on the winning side at the

Battle of Bosworth Field. The Cecil motto is the slightly Delphic '*sedo sed serio*', roughly translated as 'late but in earnest' – 'Pull the ladder up' might better fit the bill. In any event, Lord Salisbury was not being libertarian for the sake of libertarianism but for the sake of hierarchy; that is, during his time as Prime Minister, political inaction best served the rights of the propertied and well-to-do classes. Had it been otherwise, he might have used, and sometimes did, state instruments to preserve the *status quo*.

Many of the adjuncts that Lord Salisbury strengthened in support of this dispensation are, to what would be the astonishment of the reincarnated Victorian observer, still in place, even if some are a little battered. The Cecils themselves lounge gracefully yet in the home and gardens of Hatfield House, seemingly unbothered by the medieval banquets, popular classics concerts for car-driven picnickers and exhibitions of the costumes from period TV series that are now commercial mainstays of that ancient pile. The House of Lords survives as both a real and tokenistic obstacle to progress, despite its uncouth mauling by David Lloyd George before the First World War and more recent half-hearted reforms. Intriguingly, successive Marquesses of Salisbury have had a lordly hand in this process. Both Lord Salisbury's son, James, the 4th Marquess, and his grandson were, in turn, leaders of the peers, making it three Cecils in a row. The 5th Marquess of Salisbury (1893–1972), having served in the Churchill administrations, saved the hereditary peerage under the 1945–51 Attlee ministries. He successfully pleaded 'the Salisbury doctrine', exchanging relatively free passage of all manifesto commitments for aristocratic survival. It was the 6th Marquess (1916–2003) who had a spell as a Tory MP for Bournemouth and who damaged the 'One Nation' Conservative, Iain Macleod, by describing him as 'too clever by half'. His great and cerebral ancestor, the Prime Minister, had avoided that epithet in his own time by being even cleverer than that – although it should be acknowledged that the Victorians were not so adverse to brainy politicians as their descendants. The 7th Marquess backed the Salisbury Group and its journal, *The Salisbury Review*. He was MP for South Dorset from 1979 to 1987, like Bournemouth a south western seat and a reminder of Cecil influence in and around their Cranborne Manor estates in Dorset. It was he, who, when Lord Cranborne, emulated his forebears by salvaging an element of the hereditary peerage when it was under Labour threat. He brokered a deal with Tony Blair, which included the paradoxical device of peers voting for those unelected peers who should retain membership of the House. The peers always seem to find an escape clause and the United Kingdom remains one of the few democracies with a bicameral constitution the second chamber of which is unelected.

For Lord Salisbury the pinnacle of a landed-cum-moneyed upper class enjoying a major degree of political control was a landed-cum-moneyed monarchy. Vast riches and properties, ancient title and a pseudo-religious mystique were its key traits, and so it remains. Upper crust society clusters and arranges much of its social calendar around the Royal Family. Such has been the triumph of the rejuvenation of the monarchy during Lord Salisbury's rule that today there is hardly a latter-day Charles Dilke crying for a republic. It is true that the royal family may be partially enjoyed because of its newsworthy dysfunctionalism, but, then – Mrs Keppel, Mrs Simpson, Mrs Parker-Bowles – the British public have long and pruriently enjoyed regal gossip. That said, the British public does appear to be content with the notion that the headship of state should be determined by accident of birth rather than by due constitutional process.

Moreover, the monarch is sustained in the role of head of the Anglican state church. Thinking Victorians on spectral visitation to Britain would be dumbfounded. There would be widespread astonishment that the Church of England remains established and that the church is emphatically involved in great national events, such as the coronation. Lord Salisbury would be pleased to note the survival of the established church – despite the fact that the number in regular attendance at Anglican churches is no more than those for mosques, in a national population of which only 3 per cent are Muslims. He would be equally delighted to observe the continued existence of church schools. The Liberal Dissenters and secularists who laboured to build the Victorian School Boards would be profoundly shocked. A third – some 7,000 – of state schools are, to deploy the vogue term, 'faith' schools. There are 6,400 primary and 600 secondary schools, the huge majority Christian in nature. As was previously remarked, Lord Salisbury disliked the relentless logic that meant there are currently 31 Jewish, five Moslem and two Sikh schools among these. However, he would have approved of the Blair government's decision to hand over 40 state secondary schools to the Church of England, as of 2005, with a further 54 in the pipeline. Moreover, it was proposed, late in 2005, that so-called 'faith' groups, such as the innocuously named the 'United Learning Trust', might take over the independent running of schools, as part of the New Labour plan to construct what appeared to be a chaotic maelstrom of schools in the deceptively disarming name of choice and diversity. Interestingly, that aspect of the overall policy was opposed by 64 per cent in an opinion poll undertaken in 2005, this being the proportion that thought that the state should not fund 'faith' schools of any kind, a decisive assertion that the national education system should be free of any in-built sectarian or ethnic bias.

The broad-ranging approach of Lord Salisbury has stood the test of time with some fortitude. The anti-progressive weaponry examined in Chapter 6 – the Conservative Party, the House of Lords, the monarchy, the established church, church schools – are still extant. Some of their actual powers may have lessened but the potency of the imagery remains strong. Throw in another Salisbury edict – restrict democracy by keeping polling as low as possible – and the whole adds up to a picture of Lord Salisbury having strewn boulders that, 100 years on, act as obstacles to the resolution of a democratic and secular community.

The whole may be more than the sum of the parts. The maintenance of a national community where a large impoverished class are far removed, socially and culturally, from a wealthy upper echelon, has some, by no means all, its roots, in the policies pursued by Lord Salisbury. This must not be over-dramatised. Lord Salisbury did not create present-day society and would find much of it distasteful. But, at certain key points, Lord Salisbury's mark is upon it. As well as the 'social exclusion', as it is now termed, of the poorer groups, there is the deliberate and converse 'social exclusion' of many of the well-to-do classes, 6 per cent or 7 per cent of whom opt out of the universalism – the civic patriotism – of state educational and health services in favour of commercial (let us eschew the weasel words 'private' or 'independent') alternatives. Lord Salisbury would look around this scene and rejoice that the class war has not yet been lost. With his taste for 'quiddity', he would be amused by the spectacle of a Royal Family that as assiduously attends state church services as it avoids state educational and health services.

Lord Curzon, the Tory peer and Viceroy of India, called Lord Salisbury 'that strange, powerful, inscrutable and brilliant obstructive deadweight at the top'. Lord Salisbury's image is truly an ambivalent one. Lord Salisbury was not and never sought to be a popular figure and he has never really joined the gallery of Tory icons. Sir Robert Peel is remembered in the nicknames for policemen, 'Bobby' and, less memorably now, 'Peeler', while Dizzie, Winnie, Supermac and Maggie earned an adoring familiarity that Lord Salisbury never won nor craved, despite his lengthy service as Conservative Prime Minister. Outside the esoteric table talk of Oxbridge senior common rooms, his is a name that is rarely raised and, at Conservative gatherings, he is seldom recalled with affectionate and tumultuous recognition.

One of the reasons why Lord Salisbury is infrequently extolled as a Conservative hero may be his honesty. It is not merely in small details, like his haughty and, for many, still valid assessment of the *Daily Mail* – *by office boys for office boys* – that discomforts right-wingers. For all that he could be, tactically, as crafty and manipulative, even, on occasion, as deceitful as any other politician, his overall strategy was plainly outlined. He believed that society should remain hierarchical and class-oriented and that change should be avoided in defence of that ideal. He held these views sincerely and justified them with intellectual acumen. His writings, speeches and actions amount, *in toto*, to one of the frankest and most transparent expositions of the true nature of Conservatism that there has been. Unluckily for Lord Salisbury, Conservatism for the modern Conservative Party is, to recycle the words of one of Lord Salisbury's more flamboyant contemporaries, Oscar Wilde, a truth that dare not speak its name.

By office boys for office boys.

SALISBURY ON *THE DAILY MAIL*

One way of defining Lord Salisbury more clearly might be in a comparison of the first and last of the 20th century premiers. Lord Salisbury and Tony Blair share some superficial attributes. Both went to public school, although Tony Blair was not burned by a candle when a pupil, and both went to Oxford, although Lord Salisbury did not participate in the making of popular music while in residence. Both only just made it into the 20th century, with a couple of years for the former and something over two years for the latter Prime Minister. Plainly, they might be more helpfully and accurately described as the last prime minister of the 19th and the first of the 21st centuries. Both, however, have enjoyed longish phases of power.

Both statesmen have embroiled themselves in European affairs, with the 'British interest' the yardstick for any decision taken thereof, rather than any overriding devotion to European harmony as such. Both have been drawn into uncomfortable and debilitating conflicts – the Boer and Iraqi wars. Both have taken a somewhat presidential approach to their task, with Cabinet authority a secondary consideration and the House of Commons not generally acknowledged as the essential forum. Both, like Trollope's Prime Minister, Plantagenet Palliser, have been indefatigably committed to this most exacting of posts and have demonstrated high levels of intelligence and shrewdness; and, like Planty Pal, both have been fortunate in that their Lady Glencora has, like the fictional model, combined delicious foibles with fulsome strengths.

A major comparison lies in their genuine attachment not just to the Anglican Church but to its Anglo-Catholic wing. It is likely that none of the 18 intervening premiers had so strong and dedicated a faith. One might risk the guess that their religious credo pervaded their political values to a marked extent, with their conscience the final court of appeal. With this religious sense of rightness – in each case sometimes made manifest as a terrifying lack of self-doubt – central to their thinking, neither man could fairly be labelled an ideologue. Neither man proclaimed a lucid political concept of their ideal society. Indeed, both men, and it is a defensible position, resisted the dogmatism of such a creed. At its simplest, Tony Blair believes in progress and Lord Salisbury didn't, but both had cloudy viewfinders.

Lord Salisbury resisted all change. One may trace his record back and back – against all electoral reform, non-Anglicans ineligible for university or Parliament, even his ambivalence on slavery – and one begins to wonder how far back he would have travelled to find the pristine moment at which he would have believed society to be at its most desirable. For his part, Tony Blair believes mightily in change, but he does not seem to have any theoretical lodestone as to how or why and what it will look like when it is done. He has been a moderniser, not a reformer. *Punch* in early Victorian times suggested the formation of 'The Anti-meddling-in-other-people's-affairs Society'. Tony Blair has proved to be an enthusiastic meddler, where his predecessor was a reluctant one, but both have been pragmatists, not theoreticians.

Sometimes their pragmatism paid off. With Lord Salisbury's dealings with Egypt or Tony Blair's with Ireland, it was their very refusal to accept ideological and historical baggage that enabled them to find compromise solutions in extremely convoluted circumstances. There is no doubt that ideology may blind statesmen and lead them into political culs de sac. Nevertheless, it may, occasionally, be advantageous to have some guiding star by which to assess one's policies. With both premiers dangerously reliant on and finding their bearings in religious faith and personal conscience, neither ever quite clarified their political philosophies. At the risk of some disrespect to two exceptionally bright, committed and steadfastly diligent politicians, one cannot escape the feeling that Lord Salisbury did not know where he was coming from and Tony Blair did not know where he was going.

In temperament, of course, the two were at opposite poles, with Lord Salisbury the lugubrious pessimist and Tony Blair the voluble optimist. The latter has something of Voltaire's Pangloss about him, while the former is reminiscent of Mona Lott, in Tommy Handley's wartime *ITMA* programme, with her catchphrase, 'it's being so cheerful that keeps me going.' Had Karl Jung sought to personify introspection and extraversion, Lord Salisbury and Tony Blair would have made excellent visual aids. It comes as no surprise to learn that Tony Blair's favourite novel is *Ivanhoe*, where the hero successfully storms Torquilstone Castle, defeats the villainous Bois-Guilbert and lives happily ever after with the beautiful and virtuous Rowena under the benignant rule of Richard the Lionheart.

The final verdict on his great predecessor, Lord Salisbury, must eventually depend on one's political standpoint. He cannot be dismissed as a lazy or mindless or improvident or inefficient sort of politician. He proved himself, then and now, to be a highly capable and consummate political operator. Those of right-wing leanings have every right to hail him as, in thought and action, one of the purest and most devout of Conservatives. Those of left-wing sentiments must salute him, however reluctantly, as one of the most steadfast, authentic and competent of their opponents.

There are those of us who, however naively, yearn for a tolerant, serene civil society of mutual cooperation, where no one is so much richer or poorer than another that they cannot mix together, if so they wish, on tolerably good terms in common enjoyment of a decent life, where everyone has enough not only to make do but to make merry. As R H Tawney argued, 'a society is only free insofar … as its members … grow to their full stature, to do their duty as they see it, and – since liberty should not be too austere – to have their fling when they feel like it.' For such believers the legacy of Lord Salisbury is one full of impediments to the fulfilment of that outcome.

Conversely, for those who view human existence in more hierarchical and competitive terms, believing, not without some legitimate evidence, that what Lord Salisbury called the *insane passion* for equality, coupled with a heavy-handed officialdom, will destabilise communities and actually worsen conditions, and that a class-based, full-blooded individualism is the more rewarding approach, then Lord Salisbury's legacy will seem more propitious.

Even H G Wells' 'new woman', Ann Veronica, created in 1909, soon after Lord Salisbury's death, was uncertain about 'progress'; 'It still failed in something. It did seem germane to the matter that so many of the people "in the van" were plain people, or faded people, or tired-looking people. It did affect the business that they all argued badly and were egotistical in their manners and inconsistent in their phrases. There were moments when she doubted whether the whole mass of movements and societies and gatherings and talks were not simply one coherent spectacle of failure protecting itself from abjection by the glamour of its own assertions.'[2] Lord Salisbury would have applauded her insight.

One may, then, disagree with Lord Salisbury politically and yet admire him personally – or vice versa. At the last, we could do worse than turn to the considered verdict of a contemporary opponent, the Liberal politician, G W E Russell: 'of Lord Salisbury I can only observe that the combination of such genuine amiability in private life with such calculated brutality in public utterance is a psychological phenomenon which might profitably be made the subject of a Romanes lecture at Oxford.'[3]

NOTES

Chapter 1: From Noble Birth to Sitting Member

1. Quoted by A Roberts, *Salisbury: Victorian Titan* (Phoenix, London: 2000) p 10. Many of the letters and papers quoted, in this and other works, are from the Salisbury family archive kept at Hatfield House.
2. Roberts, *Salisbury*, p 26 – 'for him the two institutions were intricately intertwined'. See also M Bentley, *Lord Salisbury's World* (Cambridge University Press, Cambridge: 2001) for a clear-cut account of Lord Salisbury's beliefs about the alignment of church and state, in the section titled 'The Church'.

Chapter 2: From Stamford to Constantinople

1. Quoted at length by Roberts, *Salisbury*, p 33.
2. A full list of Lord Salisbury's journalism may be found in M Pinto-Duschinsky, *The Political Thought of Lord Salisbury* (Constable, London: 1967) pp 157–88.
3. Benjamin Disraeli, 5 August 1874 in the House of Commons; Sir Robert Ensor, in *England 1870–1914* (Oxford University Press, Oxford: 1936, latest reprint 1986) p 34, concludes 'Salisbury never entirely ceased to live up to this description'.
4. Quoted in Roberts, *Salisbury*, p 50.
5. This is quoted in D Steele, *Lord Salisbury; a Political Biography* (UCL, London: 1991) in a discussion of this policy of qualified sabre-rattling, which included his proposals about conscription. Roberts, *Salisbury*, p 170 records Lord Salisbury's description of 'English' (he

rarely used the word, 'British') policy as *floating lazily downstream, occasionally putting out a boathook to avoid diplomatic collisions* – to Lord Lytton, from the Salisbury archive.

Chapter 3: Towards the Premiership

1. Lord Salisbury, speech to the Associated Chambers of Commerce, March 1891.
2. Speech at Watford, reported in *The Times*, 5 December 1883 and cited in Roberts, *Salisbury*, p 842.

Chapter 4: Lord Salisbury Abroad

1. Lord Salisbury, 27 July 1878 at the Duke of Wellington's Riding School, now known as Knightsbridge Barracks, on the occasion of a Carlton Club banquet to celebrate the signing of the Treaty of Berlin. See Roberts, *Salisbury*, p 209.
2. Lord Salisbury, in the Prime Minister's annual Guildhall speech in London, 1895; quoted in Roberts, *Salisbury*, p 489.
3. Lord Salisbury made this remark in 1888 (see Steele, *Lord Salisbury; a Political Biography*, the section on 'Europe and Empire'). See also Ensor, *England 1870–1914*, pp 194–201, in which he concludes, rather dismissively, of Lord Salisbury, that 'he can scarcely be ranked in the first flight of international statesmen, though his place must be extremely high in the second'.
4. Quoted in Roberts, *Salisbury*, p 520.
5. Quoted in Roberts, *Salisbury*, p 518.

Chapter 5: Lord Salisbury at Home

1. Lord Salisbury, *Essays of the late Marquess of Salisbury*. These were chiefly an anthology of his vast journalistic

output, published posthumously in two volumes in 1905. This quotation is used by Steele, *Lord Salisbury; a Political Biography*.

2. Quoted in Roberts, *Salisbury*, p 684.
3. A J Mundella *Democracy and Education* (an address, undated) pp 5 and 12. See also J Lawson and H Silver, *A Social History of Education in England* (Methuen, London: 1973) Ch. X, and E Midwinter, *The Billy Bunter Syndrome; or why Britain failed to create a relevant secondary school system in the 20th century* (ContinYou, Coventry: 1998) pp 62–73.
4. Quoted in Roberts, *Salisbury*, p 500.
5. In conversation with Lady Rayleigh, 1892, quoted in Roberts, *Salisbury*, p 841.

Chapter 6: Lord Salisbury and Conservatism

1. Quoted in Roberts, *Salisbury*, p 279.
2. Quoted in Roberts, *Salisbury*, pp 114–15.
3. J P Cornford, 'The Parliamentary Foundations of the Hotel Cecil' in R Robson (ed), *Ideas and Institutions of Victorian Britain* (Barnes & Noble, New York:1967). See also J P Cornford 'The Transformation of Conservatism in the Late 19th Century' *Victorian Studies* vii (September 1963).
4. Quoted in Bentley, *Lord Salisbury's World*, the section titled 'Thought'.
5. Quoted in Roberts, *Salisbury*, p 494.
6. Quoted in Roberts, *Salisbury*, p 59.

Chapter 7: The Shorter-Term Consequences

1. *Hansard*, House of Lords, 11 June 1877.

Chapter 8: The Longer-Term Legacies

1. Lord Salisbury, in a letter to Lord Lytton dated 15 June 1877, in Lady Gwendolen Cecil, *Life of Robert, Marquess of Salisbury* (Hodder & Stoughton, London: 1921) Vol ii, Ch 4.

2. H G Wells, *Ann Veronica* (London: 1909), Ch 7 p 119 of the 2005 Penguin Classics edition.

3. G W E Russell *Sixty Years of Empire; the Queen's Prime Ministers* (Hooper & Brothers, London: 1918).

CHRONOLOGY

Year	Premiership
1900	Aged 70, Lord Salisbury begins the fifth year of his third term as Prime Minister. The Boer War: Lord Roberts named commander-in-chief of British armed forces in South Africa, Kitchener is chief of staff. The British capture Bloemfontein, relieve Mafeking, annex Orange Free State and Transvaal, and take Pretoria and Johannesburg. Ramsay MacDonald is appointed secretary of the British Labour Party. Boxer risings against Europeans in China. Australia becomes a Commonwealth.
1901	Queen Victoria dies and is succeeded by her son Edward VII. Boers begin organised guerrilla warfare; negotiations on amnesty of Cape rebels take place between Kitchener and Botha. Negotiations for Anglo-German Alliance end without agreement.
1902	Anglo-Japanese treaty recognises the independence of China and Korea. Treaty of Vereenigung ends Boer War; Orange Free State becomes British Crown Colony. 11 July: Lord Salisbury leaves office at the age of 73, having served, in three tenures the total of 13 years and 252 days as premier. He died on 22 August

History	Culture
King Umberto I of Italy is murdered by an anarchist and succeeded by his son Victor Emmanuel III. Max Planck formulates Quantum Theory.	Freud, *The Interpretation of Dreams*. Puccini, *Tosca*. Joseph Conrad, *Lord Jim*. Tolstoy, *The Living Dead*. Anton Chekhov, *Uncle Vanya*. Cezanne, *Still Life With Onions*. Sargent, *The Sitwell Family*.
US President McKinley is assassinated by an anarchist and succeeded by Theodore Roosevelt. First transatlantic radio signal transmitted.	First five Nobel Prizes awarded. Thomas Mann, *Die Buddenbrooks*. Strindberg, *Dances of Death*. Rudyard Kipling, *Kim*. Pablo Picasso's 'Blue Period' begins (–1905). Chekhov, *The Three Sisters*. Richard Strauss, *Feuersnot*.
Triple Alliance between Austria, Germany and Italy renewed for another six years. USA acquires perpetual control over Panama Canal.	Henry James, *The Ambassadors*. G E Moore, *Principia Ethica*. George Bernard Shaw, *Man and Superman*. Jack London, *The Call of the Wild*. Bruckner, *Symphony No. 9*. Film: *The Great Train Robbery*.

FURTHER READING

For Lord Salisbury's own words the most accessible anthology would be Paul Smith (ed), *Lord Salisbury on Politics; a Selection from his articles in the Quarterly Review 1860–1883* (Cambridge University Press, Cambridge: 1972).

For biographical works: Lady Gwendolen Cecil, *The Life of Robert, Marquess of Salisbury* 4 vols (Hodder & Stoughton, London: 1921, 1931, 1932) – a rather lengthy and naturally pro-Salisbury biography of invaluable resource material; Robert Taylor, *Lord Salisbury* (Allen Lane, London: 1975) is a straightforward and helpful mid-20th century account.

More recently a flurry of largely sympathetic Salisbury texts have been produced, including: David Steele, *Salisbury; a Political Biography* (UCL, London: 1999) – a well-argued study of the development of Lord Salisbury's political activities and thought; Michael Bentley, *Lord Salisbury's World* (Cambridge University Press, Cambridge: 2001) – an intelligent and well-informed thematic analysis of Lord Salisbury's political life. Andrew Roberts, *Salisbury; Victorian Titan* (Phoenix, London: 2000) – destined to be the standard major 'life', this is both comprehensively full and lucidly accessible in its friendly and well-disposed attempt to resurrect Lord Salisbury's reputation and personality.

For general background: Donald Read, *England 1868–1914* (Longmans, London: 1979) – a highly competent and juicily detailed survey of the key 'Salisbury' period; it makes for an excellent introduction to Lord Salisbury's times; R K Ensor, *England 1870–1914* (Oxford University Press, Oxford:

1936) – a magisterial and oft-reprinted volume, which, apart from offering an authoritative account of the era, is valuable in conveying the rather negative view of Lord Salisbury held during most of the 20th century.

For the salient issue of late Victorian Conservatism, the present text has leaned heavily upon: J P Cornford 'The Parliamentary Foundations of the Hotel Cecil' in R Robson (ed), *Ideas and Institutions of Victorian Britain* (Barnes & Noble, New York: 1967) – a concise and telling dissection of Lord Salisbury's Conservative Party, and E H H Green, *The Crisis of Conservatism; the politics, economics and ideology of the British Conservative Party 1880–1914* (Routledge, London: 1995) – a remarkably astute interpretation of the character and influence of the Conservative Party during and following Lord Salisbury's reign.

Finally, studies cited more incidentally include: Jose Harris, *William Beveridge; a Biography* (Clarendon, Oxford: 1997); E J Hobsbawm, *Industry and Empire* (Penguin, Harmondsworth: 1968); R H Tawney, *Equality* (4th edition 1952); R G Wilkinson, *The Impact of Inequality; how to make sick societies healthier* (Routledge, Abingdon: 2005); and Adrian Woolridge, *Measuring the Mind; Education and Psychology 1860–1990* (Cambridge University Press, Cambridge: 2005).

PICTURE SOURCES

Page vi
Photographic portrait of Lord Salisbury. Undated, by Russell, London. (Courtesy The Mary Evans Picture Library)

Pages 74–5
Lord Salisbury addressing the House of Lords, an illustration from the *Illustrated London News*, 12 March 1892. (Courtesy The Mary Evans Picture Library)

Page 111
Lord Salisbury aboard a locomobile steam car, *circa* 1902. The vehicle was limited to a range of 20 miles before its water tank had to be refilled, the condition of late 19th century roads made travel in the locomobile both hazardous and uncomfortable. (Courtesy Topham Picturepoint)

INDEX

THE 20 BRITISH PRIME MINISTERS
OF THE 20TH CENTURY

Salisbury

Balfour

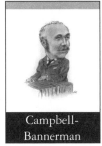

Campbell-
Bannerman

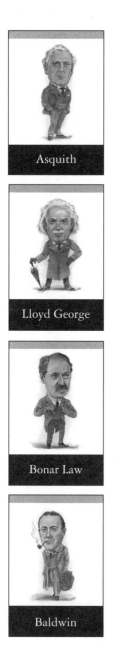

ASQUITH

His administration laid the foundation of Britain's welfare state, but he was plunged into a major power struggle with the House of Lords.

by Stephen Bates

a senior correspondent for the *Guardian*.

ISBN 1-904950-57-4 (pb)

LLOYD GEORGE

By the end of 1916 there was discontent with Asquith's management of the war, and Lloyd George schemed secretly with the Conservatives in the coalition government to take his place.

by Hugh Purcell

television documentary maker.

ISBN 1-904950-58-2 (pb)

BONAR LAW

In 1922 he was the moving spirit in the stormy meeting of Conservative MPs which ended the coalition, created the 1922 Committee and reinstated him as leader.

by Andrew Taylor

Professor of Politics at the University of Sheffield.

ISBN 1-904950-59-0 (pb)

BALDWIN

Baldwin's terms of office included two major political crises, the General Strike and the Abdication.

by Anne Perkins

a journalist, working mostly for the *Guardian*, as well as a historian of the British labour movement.

ISBN 1-904950-60-4 (pb)

MacDonald

MACDONALD

In 1900 he was the first secretary of the newly formed Labour Representation Committee (the original name for the Labour party). Four years later he became the first Labour prime minister.

by Kevin Morgan

who teaches government and politics at Manchester University.

ISBN 1-904950-61-2 (pb)

Chamberlain

CHAMBERLAIN

His name will forever be linked to the policy of appeasement and the Munich agreement he reached with Hitler.

by Graham Macklin

manager of the research service at the National Archives.

ISBN 1-904950-62-0 (pb)

Churchill

CHURCHILL

Perhaps the most determined and inspirational war leader in Britain's history.

by Chris Wrigley

who has written about David Lloyd George, Arthur Henderson and W E Gladstone.

ISBN 1-904950-63-9 (pb)

Attlee

ATTLEE

His post-war government enacted a broad programme of socialist legislation in spite of conditions of austerity. His legacy: the National Health Service.

by David Howell

Professor of Politics at the University of York and an expert in Labour's history.

ISBN 1-904950-64-7 (pb)

EDEN

His premiership will forever be linked to the fateful Suez Crisis.

by Peter Wilby

former editor of the *New Statesman*.

ISBN 1-904950-65-5 (pb)

MACMILLAN

He repaired the rift between the USA and Britain created by Suez and secured for Britain co-operation on issues of nuclear defence, but entry into the EEC was vetoed by de Gaulle in 1963.

by Francis Beckett

author of BEVAN, published by Haus in 2004.

ISBN 1-904950-66-3 (pb)

DOUGLAS-HOME

Conservative politician and prime minister 1963-4, with a complex career between the two Houses of Parliament.

by David Dutton

who teaches History at Liverpool University.

ISBN 1-904950-67-1 (pb)

WILSON

He held out the promise progress, of 'the Britain that is going to be forged in the white heat of this revolution'. The forced devaluation of the pound in 1967 frustrated the fulfilment of his promises.

by Paul Routledge

The *Daily Mirror's* chief political commentator.

ISBN 1-904950-68-X (pb)

Heath

HEATH

A passionate European, he succeeded during his premiership in effecting Britain's entry to the EC.

by Denis MacShane

Minister for Europe in Tony Blair's first government.

ISBN 1-904950-69-8 (pb)

Callaghan

CALLAGHAN

His term in office was dominated by industrial unrest, culminating in the 'Winter of Discontent'.

by Harry Conroy

When James Callaghan was Prime Minister, Conroy was the Labour Party's press officer in Scotland, and he is now editor of the Scottish *Catholic Observer.*

ISBN 1-904950-70-1 (pb)

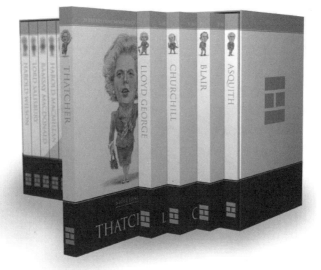

Thatcher

THATCHER
Britain's first woman prime minister and the longest serving head of government in the 20th century (1979–90), but also the only one to be removed from office in peacetime by pressure from within her own party.
by Clare Beckett
teaches social policy at Bradford University.
ISBN 1-904950-71-X (pb)

Major

MAJOR
He enjoyed great popularity in his early months as prime minister, as he seemed more caring than his iron predecessor, but by the end of 1992 nothing seemed to go right.
by Robert Taylor
is Research Associate at the LSE's Centre for Economic Performance.
ISBN 1-904950-72-8 (pb)

Blair

BLAIR
He is therefore the last prime minister of the 20th century and one of the most controversial ones, being frequently accused of abandoning cabinet government and introducing a presidential style of leadership.
by Mick Temple
is a senior lecturer in Politics and Journalism at Staffordshire University.
ISBN 1-904950-73-6 (pb)

THE 20 BRITISH PRIME MINISTERS
OF THE 20TH CENTURY

www.hauspublishing.co.uk

KIPLING
by Jad Adams
ISBN 1-904950-19-1 (hb)

The personal life of Rudyard Kipling intersected with more than one 20th century prime minister. Stanley Baldwin was his cousin, an early source of envy and inspiration. But it was Herbert Asquith's path that Kipling crossed at the critical point in his career.

For just as Asquith made his legal reputation as a deadly forensic cross-examiner in the Parnell Inquiry, Kipling helped consolidate his own reputation with the angry verse he wrote in response to Asquith's clearing of Parnell, establishing Kipling as the voice of what for many became a certain ideal of Britishness. But as Jad Adams' biography reveals, there was always paradox behind the ideal.

Kipling, the voice of British India? In fact Kipling spent only 12 of his 70 years in India and left the subcontinent for the last time when he was 25. Kipling, the laureate of the English? In fact he was never happier than in the years he spent with his young family and American wife in Vermont. Kipling the idoliser of masculine action and soldierly deeds? In reality Kipling was so myopically unathletic that he was rejected as unfit for military service.

And above all there was the childhood. *Kim, Stalky & Co.*, the *Jungle Book*, and many more child-centered stories testify to Kipling's lifelong identification with the freedoms and creativity of childhood – yet in Kipling's own childhood there is a terrible blank. There was separation from his parents, from India, and from hope. It was that, writes Adams, that was the source foundation of the 'deep wound of loneliness and rejection' in Kipling's soul, a wound that may be the key to the strangeness and the continuing appeal of the Kipling world.

PANKHURST
by Jad Adams
ISBN 1-904341-53-5 (pb)

Emmeline Pankhurst led, and to this day personifies, the Women's Suffrage movement. It was as founder and leader of the WSPU that she has come to ubiquitously symbolise the struggle for the women's vote in Britain. It was the WSPU motto, 'Deeds not words', that, from its founding in Pankhurst's home in 1903, differentiated the WSPU from the other, more benign Suffrage movements.

Jad Adams ably and clearly charts the incremental influence and growing radicalism of both Pankhurst and the WSPU, from their first acts of spontaneous militancy in 1905 to their later imprisonment and hunger strikes. They sought to force Women's Suffrage onto a reluctant Asquith's national agenda, using all means possible including blowing up Lloyd George's home.

What Pankhurst lacked as a far-sighted strategist, she compensated for with an infectious charisma and conviction, often both encouraging and condoning random acts of sporadic militancy by WSPU members. Calls from within the WSPU to democratise the organisation in 1907 were met with the response: 'I shall tear up the constitution'; such was the autocratic nature of her leadership.

Adam's paints an intriguing picture of a self-promoting and self-sacrificing woman, but one who was ultimately wholly consumed and motivated by the injustice of a system she set out, and succeeded, to change. This challenging biography clearly charts the suffrage movement from its incarnation, and re-examines the complex legacy of Pankhurst's life.

WILDE

by Jonathan Fryer

ISBN 1-904341-11-X (pb)

The undisputed Victorian master of the *bon mot* reserved the best one to describe his on life: 'I have put my talent into writing, my genius I have saved for living.' – Wilde on Wilde.

Born in the middle of the 19th century, he was simultaneously a product of his era and far ahead of his time, in fact an impressively modern figure. His predilection for sartorial extravagance and his unusual, as well as excessive lifestyle are probably the best known and most commented on facets of this man about town. He himself flaunted this uniqueness: 'There is only one thing in the world worse than being talked about, and that is not being talked about.' Becoming an acid critic of society he soon gained himself a reputation as a slayer of the dragons of pomposity, hypocrisy and cant of his age. His rise as talented and acclaimed playwright and novelist seemed unstoppable. But as spectacular as his rise so was his fall: a trial, a sentence, a prison-term. After that exile and his name only mentioned in a scandalised whisper.

Similar to Lord Salisbury he represents the Victorian era. Wilde dies towards the end of the term of the first Prime Minister of the 20th century, on 30 November 1900. Since his death many different critical evaluations have been made both of the writer and of the man. Jonathan Fryer offers a fresh look, an entertaining introduction and well-informed summary of this extraordinary person, as well as of the different critical approaches to his life and work.